FROM THE GROUND UP

AN AUTOBIOGRAPHY

FROM THE GROUND UP

AN AUTOBIOGRAPHY

VIOLA MACMILLAN

ECW PRESS

NATIONAL LIBRARY OF CANADA CATALOGUING IN PUBLICATION DATA

Viola MacMillan
From the ground up: an autobiography

ISBN 1-55022-457-3

1. MacMillan, Viola. 2. Women miners — Canada — Bioraphy. 3. Businesswomen —
Canadian — Biography. 1. Title.

TN140.M25A3 2001   622'.'092   C00-933262-6

Edited by Tracey Millen
Cover and text design by Tania Craan
Layout by Mary Bowness

Printed by Transcontinental

Distributed in Canada by
General Distribution Services,
325 Humber College Blvd.,
Toronto, ON, M9W 7C3

Published by ECW PRESS
2120 Queen Street East, Suite 200
Toronto, ON M4E 1E2
ecwpress.com

This book is set in Sabon and Penumbra.

PRINTED AND BOUND IN CANADA

The publication of *From the Ground Up* has been generously supported by the
Canada Council, the Ontario Arts Council and the Government of Canada through
the Book Publishing Industry Development Program. Canadä

INTRODUCTION

Several publishers urged Viola MacMillan to tell her story while she was still alive. They knew her autobiography would sell because it had so many elements of intrigue: the metamorphosis of farm girl into powerful businesswoman, the triumph of tenacity over gender, and finally, like icing on a cake, a jailed protagonist. But MacMillan refused to co-operate. Already publicity shy, she was so scarred by her role in a 1960s' mining scandal that the idea of any more press, even positive press, was repellant to her.

It wasn't until MacMillan reached her 80s that publishing legend Jack McClelland, former president of the Canadian publishing house McClelland & Stewart and an acquaintance of MacMillan's, persuaded her to hire a ghostwriter before it was too late. He suggested Philip Smith, a published author who specialized in historical non-fiction and was knowledgeable about the mining industry. Based on extensive interviews with MacMillan, Smith completed an autobiography entitled *From the Ground Up*. MacMillan not only refused to have the manuscript published but wouldn't allow anyone, not even her closest friends, to read it.

Instead, the unpublished work yellowed amongst her voluminous collection of papers until MacMillan's death in August,

1993, at the age of 90. During the posthumous scramble to organize her affairs and archive her papers, the executors of MacMillan's estate rediscovered the manuscript and read it. Although the tale needed amplification, the executors agreed that Smith had captured MacMillan's indomitable spirit in his writing. The tapes of Smith's interviews were lost and Smith himself died in 1996, but his edited manuscript forms the basis for the autobiography you are about to read.

From the Ground Up is a chronological account of MacMillan's exceptional life: her underprivileged upbringing in Ontario's cottage country; her determined efforts to escape the farm and pursue a "glamorous" career as a stenographer; her first introduction to prospecting, her rise to fame as a successful miner and lobbyist; her downfall at the hands of securities regulators; and, later, her vindication. The tale is made all the more powerful by MacMillan's portrayal of the extraordinary as ordinary and her refusal to view her gender as a handicap to success in a man's world. She had a magic touch, or maybe just a supreme air of confidence, that rendered associates oblivious to her sex. In this understated way she rose to the top of an industry that, half-a-century later, is still dominated by men.

But the Windfall Affair, a well-publicized mining scandal in which MacMillan played a leading role, was a painful subject that she chose to avoid. The scandal stemmed from one borehole drilled near the huge Texas Gulf copper-zinc discovery in northern Ontario in July, 1964, by Windfall Oil and Mines, one of MacMillan's exploration companies. Windfall's share price skyrocketed on speculation of a major find, but crashed within the month when the drill core was found to be barren. Public outcry over trading losses led to a Royal Commission investigation. MacMillan and her husband George were charged with fraud. They were acquitted a few years later, but not before a 64-year-old MacMillan became the first person in Canada to be jailed on a peripherally related charge of "wash trading," the act of trading shares in order to create the appearance of market activity in a stock.

Although MacMillan's autobiography presents her side of the

controversial story, it says little about why she was singled out for punishment or about the behind-the-scenes machinations that touched the entire Canadian securities industry. To provide context for the story and fill in some of the gaps, Virginia Heffernan, a mining journalist, returned to MacMillan's papers archived at the Canadian Museum of Nature and interviewed several of MacMillan's contemporaries. The results of Heffernan's research are presented in an Afterword that follows *From the Ground Up*.

CHAPTER ONE

In the very year I was born, which was 1903, a blacksmith named Fred La Rose, working on the railroad being built to open up northern Ontario, came across a vein of silver in a rock cut. That discovery, in the wilderness where the town of Cobalt soon sprang up, was one of the greatest things that ever happened to the Canadian mining industry. In turn, that industry has created many billions of dollars in new riches for this country.

Through the years, more than a hundred mines were developed around Cobalt. All told they produced almost half a billion ounces of silver worth hundreds of millions of dollars. And perhaps what is even more important was that Cobalt became a sort of cradle for the Canadian mining industry. Some of the most important men in the business, men I would come to know well in later years, learned their trade there. They later fanned out to put their knowledge to use all over this country, and a good part of the rest of the world.

Fred La Rose's discovery was important for me, too, in an indirect sort of way. It was years later in Cobalt that I caught mining fever and determined to make my career in the business. That career earned me a bigger fortune than I could ever have imagined as a little girl growing up on the farm. I also gained a certain amount of fame, and even in the saddest episode of my whole life, more notoriety than I thought I could stand.

Because I made my career in an industry that is still, even today, almost entirely a man's world, many people through the years have urged me to write my life story. Somehow, I always seemed too busy to get down to it. But in today's world, where what they call "women's issues" always seem to be making news, perhaps it is time for me to go over my scrapbooks and newspaper clippings, dig into my memory, and tell how life was for me.

People have often asked me if men resented my success in the business world. Some of them may have. Success doesn't come easily, and often those who don't find it become envious of those who do. But on the whole, most of the men I met encouraged me in whatever I tried to do, and many of them helped me a great deal along the way.

I always believed that women could do anything men could, if they were just prepared to put their minds to it and get down to work. Perhaps it was unusual that I became a prospector, and countless newspaper and magazine stories were written about my life in the bush. But I didn't see anything strange in it, and the fact that I was elected president of the Prospectors and Developers Association for 21 years in a row goes to show that mining men didn't either.

Anyway, my life began 86 years ago on a little farm at Deebank, in that Muskoka Lakes area which is now vacation-land for thousands of families from Toronto and the other cities in southern Ontario. Beautiful though my home country was and still is now, the land is too hilly and rocky to make a farmer's life there all milk and honey. There were certainly no vacations for my father and mother, or us kids as we grew up. I was the 13th of my father's 15 children, which is perhaps why, unlike most people, I consider the number 13 to be a lucky one. But perhaps I'd better start at the beginning.

For many years, our family knew little or nothing about our father's father, who died long before I was born. But lately my nephew Ross and his wife have been doing some research into the family tree. From this it seems that my grandfather, Richard J. Huggard, was a carpenter who emigrated from Ireland in 1847, at around the age of 31. Richard settled first at Butternut Ridge, in King's County, New Brunswick. He was evidently a hardworking and thrifty man, and three years later he was able to bring his wife Mary and their five-year-old son Joseph over to Canada to join him. Richard and Mary had six more children, including my father Thomas, the first to be born in this country. He came along in 1853, so he was already middle-aged when I arrived on the scene.

For some reason my grandfather and his wife split up, and he and a couple of his friends journeyed to Ontario where they became the first homesteaders in the Deebank area in 1862. My father was then nine, and I guess my grandfather figured he was old enough to help on the farm, because he took him along to Deebank. Mary kept the younger children, and we think they all headed for the west. We don't know for sure, because my father never heard from his mother or any of his brothers and sisters ever again. That was a great sadness for him, and he never got over it. Sometimes he would sit in the corner of our kitchen, trying not to let us see him wiping tears from his eyes when he thought about them.

Though he was very short like me, my father was tough and wiry and very handsome. He was a widower with three children when he married my mother, Harriet Spiers, whose father was a pioneer settler at Huntsville. Though Huntsville is no more than an hour's drive from Deebank now, it must have seemed an awful long way away in those horse-and-buggy days. However, young Harriet (she was only 18 at the time) settled in to raise her husband's three children and begin a family of her own.

Like my father, my mother was short and stocky, but very strong, and a bundle of energy. And she needed to be, because her life was just one long round of work. Thirteen years younger than my father, she was only nine years older than Elizabeth, the eldest of the three stepchildren she inherited. And only a year after she took on the task of caring for this young family, so far away from her own folks, she had the first of her own 12 children, my oldest brother George. That was in 1885, and she had eight more children

— three boys and five girls — before I was born. She would then be 37 years old, but five years later she had my brother Ed — and four years after that, when she was 46, my brother Reg completed the family.

I guess I should be grateful to my parents for my tough genes, but as I began to grow up I wasn't at all grateful for the names they gave me. They christened me Violet Rita, and when I began to go to school all the kids used to make fun of my name, as I guess all kids everywhere like to do. "Roses are red, Violets are blue," they would chant. Crazy stuff to get worked up about, but when I left home later I took care to have people call me Viola, which I thought sounded much nicer.

I have travelled a lot during my lifetime. In my heyday, when airplanes were a lot slower than they are today, I was regularly logging 30,000 miles a year. I suppose I got into the habit of moving around early. When I was only nine days old, my father moved to another farm about halfway between Deebank and Windermere, one of the loveliest spots in the Muskokas. Because of its location on Lake Rosseau, Windermere was settled about 20 years before Deebank, in the 1840s. And by the time I was born it had already become popular with summer vacationers.

I don't remember anything about the move, of course, but I've been told my mother carried me in her arms along the trail leading to our new place. I don't remember much about our life there, either, because when I was four years old my father left one of my brothers, Bert, who would have been about 18 at the time, in charge of that place, while he went out and bought a new farm right in Windermere.

Just about the earliest memory I have is the day of that second move. We had to cross a hill we called Beech Ridge, and I was too small to walk all that way by myself, so my brother Joe carried me on his shoulders. Joe would have been 15 then, and it was not long before he left home and found a job in the Coniagas mine in Cobalt. He didn't come home much after that, but when he did, he used to tell me so many stories about his life underground that I worshipped him as a great adventurer.

I've spoken earlier about my father's sadness over his separation from his family, and my mother had a similar sadness in her life, because even though my father worked hard, our place was too small to support a large family. As my older brothers and sisters grew up, all except Bert had to leave home to find work. My mother never wanted them to go, and I'm sure they found the break so painful that they usually just ran away, and it might be days or weeks before my mother heard where they had fetched up. She must have shed a lot of tears over them, but she never let us younger kids know about that. Instead, she just buried herself in work.

Our new farm was right next to Windermere House, which is today one of the poshest resort hotels in the Muskokas. Even then, when I suppose you would have called it a lodge, it was popular with vacationers from the city. Somehow, with all her other activities, my mother managed to get the cleaning contract there. How she did it all I don't know. My father had a contract to deliver the mail, by horse and buggy in the summer and sleigh in the winter, but more often than not it would be my mother who would do the rounds. She was also the local midwife, though she didn't have any medical training. She would just put on her long white apron and go to work, sometimes with a doctor around, but not always.

Once, when I was about 15, my mother couldn't go on a case so our local doctor took me along to stand in for her. He watched quietly enough as I delivered the baby. I must say the mother did most of the work, but when I had finished cleaning up the newborn he said briskly: "You'll never be as good as your mother. You didn't pound that child hard enough on the back to get it breathing." Right there and then, I decided whatever future career I had, it would definitely not be midwifery.

I had a list once of all the children my mother brought into this world, and there were more than 200 names on it. And when she wasn't working outside the house, she would be hard at it inside. Her sewing machine would be chattering away most evenings, and it may sound corny today, but she really did make pants for me and my sister Sadie out of flour bags, and petticoats out of sugar bags. Our dresses were usually hand-me-downs from the summer visitors, which she would alter to fit us.

Sadie was a year older than me, and when we started school we had to walk two miles every morning to Deebank. That was nice in the spring and fall, but I still shudder to think of those bitterly cold Muskoka mornings. Later, my father was one of the leaders of a group that managed to get a one-room school going in Windermere. My mother landed the cleaning contract for that, too. So I wound up as a sort of unpaid caretaker. I would have to start up the fires in the morning and clean up in the afternoon after everyone left. There was a lady living across from the school, Mrs. Tom Smith. She used to feel sorry for me, and would call me in every afternoon after I had finished cleaning up, and give me a slice of white bread with white sugar on it. That was a real luxury for me, because we only had my mother's brown bread at home.

I guess I was a bit of a hellion at school. My best friend was Celia Klingbeil. Her father bought the farm I moved from when I was nine days old, and I believe it is still in their family. Celia and I loved to wrestle, and we would wrestle with the boys, too. I would get baseball games going — well, we called it baseball, but I suppose the way we played it was more like what English girls call "rounders."

The only time I ever had for playing was when I was at school. There was always too much work to do at home on the farm. It was a mixed farm, of the kind you don't see too much today. We had a few cows, pigs, chickens, and of course the horses. My favourites were the sheep. I remember the first animal I ever saw being born: a darling little lamb. It was after our Methodist Sunday School class, up in one of the back pastures. That lamb became the nearest thing I ever had to a pet, and, oh my, how I cried when it had to go to market!

My father taught me how to milk the cows when I was very little, and that was a regular chore I had to do before I went off to school. I worked with the horses, too. I wouldn't have won any awards for dressage or anything like that, but I could handle them. I must have looked really comical perched on their backs. I was tinier than the smallest jockey, and of course our work horses were much bigger than thoroughbreds. But I would climb up on the manger to get on their backs, and when I wanted to get off, I would guide them over to a fence or gate and clamber down that way.

Summers, of course, were our busiest times. After the spring ploughing and seeding, there would be hay to be cut and stooked and grain to be brought in. And of course my mother would be at her busiest then at Windermere House. I suppose I would have been nine or ten when she began to take Sadie and me to help her, down on our hands and knees scrubbing the pine floors. And sometimes, on evenings when the guests would have dances at the lodge, Sadie and I would creep up onto the porch and peek inside. It all seemed so glamorous to me. I couldn't have been more thrilled if I had been peeking into a ballroom in one of those old European palaces, watching the lords and ladies dancing minuets and bowing to each other under the chandeliers.

There were already cottagers in Windermere by then, too, and another of my chores, after milking the cows, would be to deliver their daily orders for milk and cream. I remember one morning, well before eight o'clock, I was carrying a quart of milk and a quarter of a pint of cream to a couple who came up from Toronto every summer. I was expecting to meet their daughter, as usual. Instead, I was greeted by a Chinese servant they had brought up with them. He had this long pigtail down his back and a funny little black hat on top of his head. I had never seen anything like that before. He could have been a Martian for all I knew. And I was so terrified, that I just dropped the milk and ran all the way home, barefoot as I was. It was a long time before I would go back there.

But I was always so glad to see all the summer visitors, and they were very good to us. I remember once a lady gave Sadie and me a doll each. We were so excited we ran home to show them to our mother. But we weren't allowed to play with them like other kids did. My mother put ribbons on them, and hung them up in opposite corners of the living room as ornaments.

A lot of Americans used to stay at Windermere House. I remember one man, a big bearded fellow. I think his name was Colonel Ben High. He always wanted to see "that little black-eyed-little-gal," as he called me, and he would give me five cents or a dime whenever we met. And there were two professors who used to stay at the hotel, with their wives. They had a college in, I think it was Indiana, and once they tried to persuade my father to let them take me back with them. "This little girl must have an education," they told him. I thought they were crazy, talking to my father like that. And there was certainly no way he was about to let me go.

The year 1914 was a tragic one for the whole world, of course, with the outbreak of what we then called the Great War. And it was a bad year for us, too. One day in April, a spark flew out of the chimney and set fire to the roof of our house. We had just finished dinner. We always ate our main meal at midday, and I had tucked my youngest brother Reg in bed upstairs for his afternoon nap. As soon as I realized the house was on fire, I ran upstairs to get him. He wasn't two years old yet, and he could crawl but not walk. And he was a big fat kid, far too heavy for me to carry. So I just dragged him down the stairs and pulled him outside, where I left him, safe as I thought, on a big flat rock.

Then I ran back inside the house to rescue the only three little treasures I owned. These were a cup and saucer I had gotten as a gift on the Christmas tree one year (I still have them), a scrap of a curtain I had bought for my mother, and a tiny doll's trunk. It was terrifying how fast the fire spread. My mother almost got caught inside the house, because she was running around trying frantically to find Reg. Then we discovered that while I was back inside the house, one of our neighbours, Mrs. Forge, had rescued him from his perch on the rock and taken him into her house.

So we all got out alive, but we lost everything in the blaze. Our neighbours rallied round to help, giving us clothes and things, and we moved into the large driving shed where we normally kept the buggies and democrats. We lived there all that summer, while my father built us a new house. This time he was determined it would not burn down and he built it with cement blocks. I helped him make them, using gravel that we had on our other farm.

Before the new house was ready for us, my mother cooked on an old wood stove in the shed. And it was while we were living like that, that I had an experience I still shudder to think about. My mother and father had gone away somewhere for the day, and left me to cook dinner for some men we had working on the farm. Before he left, my father cut the head off a chicken — he knew I could never kill a chicken — and left me to clean it and cook it. I managed to pluck the bird all right, but I just couldn't bring myself to reach inside it and clean it. So I just dumped it into the big iron pot and boiled it all up together. I don't know whether the men noticed anything strange about their meal. If they did, they were too polite to mention it. But I have never relished chicken to this day, and I've had to eat a lot of it at formal banquets through the years.

As if losing our house was not a big enough setback for my father, he suffered another blow in August that same year. An excursion boat came into Windermere for the day, and a group of the passengers asked my father if they could go and get some rabbits from underneath our barn. He must have regretted it later, but he was a kindly man and he gave them permission. And didn't the damn fools go looking for the rabbits with matches!

Well, if you've ever seen a barn go up in smoke, you know what a frightening sight it is. It was all over in a few minutes; so fast that my father couldn't rescue a team of horses he had stabled inside. I was too young to know anything about insurance and things like that in those days, but I doubt my father ever got repaid for that loss. I'm ready to bet those fool excursionists just thought it was all a great lark.

CHAPTER TWO

By 1915, three of my brothers had enlisted and gone away to the war: Bert, Jim, and the one I guess I was closest to, my idol, Joe. With Bert no longer around to help with the work, my father was in real trouble. He was in his early 60s by then, and he had had a heart attack a few years earlier. So my mother and father decided I had to leave school and join my sister Sadie, working full-time on the farm.

I was only 12, and I was very unhappy about it. I had finished the junior fourth grade, but I still had one more year to go in senior fourth, before I could sit the entrance examination for high school. And I desperately wanted to do that, because by now I was bound and determined I was going to be a stenographer. The summer visitors had made me realize there was a great big exciting world outside Windermere, and I wanted one day to be part of it. Some of the lady visitors were stenographers, and that seemed to me a very glamorous thing to be.

Another reason why I was so set on getting an education, was because I felt so sorry for my father. He never had a day's schooling in his life, and he couldn't read or write. So when a letter came from one of my brothers, I would have to read it to him. And he could never get enough news about the war, so I would have to read the newspapers to him. My mother could read a little bit, and write, but she was always too busy to read to my father. My sister Sadie would also read to him sometimes, but she was too impatient to finish the stories. My father would sometimes get mad when he heard from one of his friends, some news item Sadie had not bothered to read to him.

So even though I had to leave school, I vowed that one day I would go back and complete my education. I knew my mother didn't want me to leave home at all, but I kept my school books, wrapped them up in paper, and tied the bundle with binder twine. Then I hid it up in the attic where my little brothers and Sadie couldn't find it.

Every year after that, when the kids from my school set off on the 25-mile journey to Bracebridge in June to sit their high school entrance exam, they would have to pass our place, and I would cry my eyes out because I couldn't go with them. I remember one year, when my parents had sent me down to the cellar to sort the potatoes they kept in a big bin — I had to pick out any that felt soft, to prevent them from spoiling the others — when the kids went by on their way to Bracebridge, all excited, I was so sad that I took the rotten potatoes and just hurled them as far as I could across the road.

I suppose I knew more about the war than other kids my age, because of having to read the news to my father. And it seemed to drag on forever. But I remember how happy we all were when it ended. Sadie and I were shoveling gravel that day, from the pit on my father's other farm. Our little brother Ed was trying to help us, but he was only ten and not much use. The pit was so deep that we had to put another team of horses on to haul the cart out of it. But we drew down ten cartloads that day, took them to the dock in Windermere, and loaded them onto a scow to be ferried across the lake for construction work at Lady Eaton's summer place.

That evening, my father was so happy that the war was over, and all his boys had survived it, that he had us go and collect a pile of brush and logs for a huge bonfire. And he got one of his old suits and stuffed it with straw. That was Kaiser Bill, and people came from miles around to see us burn him. One boy from a farm about 12 or 15 miles away looked at me a bit strangely. I looked at him, too, and that's about where I first started to look at boys.

My father's happiness at the end of the war didn't last long. Joe had no sooner returned to his wife and two children in Cobalt, than he took sick and died in the great epidemic of Spanish flu that the soldiers brought back with them from France. My father had his body brought home to be buried in the family plot at Ullswater, but they couldn't bring the casket in the house because everyone was so scared of the way the flu was spreading. Instead, they left it in the drive-shed overnight. I just felt awful about that.

Early in 1919, with Bert back on the farm, I took the bull by the horns. Occasionally during the war, when my father would be having his tea in the afternoon (he was always tired out by about four o'clock), he would look at Sadie and me and say sadly, "whatever's going to become of you girls?" Sadie wasn't at all interested in getting an education. In that day and age, most girls just took it as natural that they would grow up to be housewives and mothers. Education was for boys. But somehow I had set my sights on something different. When my father talked like that I would stamp my foot and say, "Dad, you know very well what I'm going to do. I'm going back to school." I knew I had to do that if I was going to have any hope of being a stenographer.

When Bert settled back into the farm routine, I figured this was the time, and I started agitating again. Eventually, my father said, "Well, if you're determined to go back to school you'll have to, but you'll have to get all your chores done in the morning before you go." I was so excited that I dashed up to the attic for my books, unwrapped them, took them downstairs, and put them on my mother's sewing machine. She was away on the stage with the mail, and when she came in she saw them and said, "What are they there for?" I said, "I'm going back to school tomorrow." She said, "No you're not." Of course, she knew very well that if I passed my high school entrance exam, I would leave home like all her other children, and she dearly wanted me to stay with her.

But I was determined, and that evening, just at supper time, I walked down the hill to the teacher's place. Her name was Edna Hough. She married a farmer later, and I kept in touch with her for years. She lived with her mother, and two younger brothers who were still going to the school. When she realized that I wanted to talk about something important, Edna took me upstairs to her room so we wouldn't be interrupted by her kid brothers.

The entrance exam was only about three months away, but I told Edna that if she would let me back into the school, I would work really hard and I was sure I would pass. She said, "Oh no, Violet." Oh, how I hated that name! "You've been away from school for three years now, and I don't think you could possibly catch up a whole year's work by June. Besides, there are some questions on the exam about history, and you're not very good in history."

I had to admit that was true, and I wasn't very good at geography either, for that matter. But I had always been okay at composition and math, and I pleaded with her to let me join the entrance class. I told her that if she would only help me, I would do anything she wanted me to, and I was sure I could catch up. Even back then, I knew that if you wanted something you had to work hard to get it, and by that time I knew all about hard work. But Edna was still doubtful and didn't think she'd be able to put my name forward for the entrance.

I was so disappointed I burst into tears and rushed out of her room. When I got downstairs, Edna's mother saw my red eyes and asked me whatever was the matter. I was sobbing so hard I couldn't even answer her. And when Edna followed me down and realized how badly I felt, she changed her mind and agreed to let me back into the school. "But," she told me, "you've got to work very hard, Violet. You have a lot of subjects to catch up on."

I was so happy! "Oh, I'll work hard all right," I told her. "You just tell me what to do and I'll do it." I was always good at that. If I had to do something, I'd do it, somehow. And Edna really helped me when I got back into the classroom. She would lend me books to take home after school. Of course, I didn't dare let my mother see me reading them. But at night, after the farm chores were done, I would study in my bedroom until one, two, or three in the morning. And to make sure my mother didn't see the oil lamp alight in my room, I would pin the window blinds to the sides of the frame, and cover the crack at the bottom of the door with my clothes.

I really studied hard for those three months, and when the time came, Edna agreed to let me go to Bracebridge to sit my entrance exam. Oh, that was really something for me, to be away from home for three days, in the biggest town I had ever seen! It could have been New York City, in my eyes.

I went home not knowing whether I had passed the exam, of course, and there I received the biggest surprise of my young life. My father had sold his main farm to a group of well-to-do Toronto people, who turned it into what is now the Windermere Golf and Country Club, right across the road from Windermere House. And with the money he received (I think it was something like $6,000), he had bought Fife House, a little hotel in the village.

Well, that was exciting news, of course, but not as exciting to me as when my name appeared in the paper as having passed my entrance exam. There was no high school in Windermere, and I didn't know how I was going to manage it, but I vowed that when September came around, I would be going to high school some place.

First, though, there was the summer to be worked in the hotel. I think now, that one of the reasons my father bought it was to try to keep me at home. Anyway, I handled all the letters from people making inquiries and booked the reservations. I had the guests sign the register when they arrived, and saw them off when they left, making sure they had settled their bills, of course. And Sadie and I would scrub the floors, clean the guests' rooms, and wait on tables. I loved meeting the guests, although some of the men made me mad by cleaning their boots on the towels, which we had to wash by hand.

As with most family businesses, at least in those days, Sadie and I didn't expect to be paid wages. But we did get tips, and I saved mine until I had six dollars, which I used to buy a trunk, even though I didn't have nearly enough clothes to fill it. My mother must have known then that it was all over. I was going away to school. So it was arranged that I would go to North Bay and stay with my eldest stepsister, Elizabeth, who had married a man named Dreany, and had a grown-up family.

When the time came for me to leave, at the end of the summer holiday season, I had to go to the train station at Utterson, about 20 miles from our place, where we used to go to pick up the mail. My father drove me there in a democrat, one of those old two-seat buggies, with my half-empty trunk tied on the back. And I know that even though he sympathized with my desire to get an education, he was very sad that I was leaving. He thought the world of me. He thought there was nobody smarter than me. I think he particularly liked me because I used to talk back to him. And if I thought he was doing something he shouldn't be doing, I used to scold him unmercifully.

And me? At the age of 16 I was scared to death about going all that way on the train alone. I think the journey took about three hours, but it seemed much longer than that to me. My father had warned me not to talk to any strange men on the train, and he must have been as nervous as I was when the train pulled out and he stood on the platform waving to me.

Years later, I heard a naughty story that reminded me of how I must have been on that train trip. It seems there was a gentleman on a train reading a magazine. When he had finished it he took pity on a young girl travelling alone like I was. "Would you like to see my Cosmopolitan?" he asked her. "Sir," she cried, "you undo one button and I'll call the porter."

Well, I didn't have to call the porter, but I was so relieved when Elizabeth met me in the station at North Bay. And from then on, she was like a second mother to me. She had a nice house, and was a very religious person. My father always used to say, "Well. There's one who'll go to Heaven anyway."

I lived with Lizzie for about three months, but I never did get to go to high school. Since I was still determined to be a stenographer, it was decided I should enroll in the local business college. And so I started to learn about typing and Pitman's shorthand.

But the fees were $13.50 a month, and with the hotel closed for the season, my father ran out of funds after I had been at the college only two months.

Obviously, I was going to have to find a job somewhere. But there didn't seem to be any jobs available in North Bay at that time. Rescue came in the form of a letter from one of Elizabeth's sons, Leonard Dreany, who was living with his wife in Windsor. I was Leonard's aunt, even though he was so much older than me. And he said in his letter that the Motor City, as it was already being called, was booming. There were plenty of jobs there, and if I wanted to, I could go and live with him until I was settled in and able to make my own way.

So once again I got on the train. My journey this time took me almost past our place in the Muskokas, and I felt very homesick as the train puffed along on its way to Toronto. The Queen City in 1919 was a much smaller place than it is today, with nary a sky-scraper to be seen. The Royal York Hotel now stands across the street from Union Station. It was in this hotel that I would in later years spend many fruitful and happy hours, but at the time was not even built yet. But the huge Union Station, and all the bustle out-side, were enough to frighten the life out of me, and I had several hours to wait for my connection to Windsor.

One of the summer visitors who had been kind to me back home had given me her address and telephone number and told me if ever I was in Toronto I must look her up. That had seemed an unlikely prospect at the time, but here I was, alone and very lonely in Union Station. So I called her. She was delighted and started to give me directions to her place, which streetcar to take, and so on. But I was far too terrified to venture out into the busiest streets I had ever seen in my short life. I just knew I'd get lost and miss my connection. Realizing how scared I was, the lady dropped every-thing and came down to the station to meet me. I was so relieved to see someone I knew that I must have chattered her ear off. But she stayed with me, and saw me onto my train for the next stage of the journey.

Now, I thought, I was safe. All I had to do was sit tight and

Leonard would meet me at Windsor. But there was some kind of washout on the railroad track and instead the train wound up in Detroit. At that time, you had to be vaccinated to get into the United States, so there was another hold up for that, and I have the mark on my arm to this day. How Leonard ever found me, his tiny little aunt scared stiff in a foreign country, I don't know. But he did, and he drove me home to begin my new life in Windsor.

Just as Leonard had said in his letters, there was plenty of work in the Motor City, though the cars they were building in those days were a far cry from the ones we see speeding along the expressways nowadays. The first job I found was in a department store, unpacking and washing dishes before they were put on display for sale. That didn't pay very much, of course, but it wasn't long before I found a better one, at Bell Telephone. By the time I had taken the operator's course, some supervisor there had decided I was good at dealing with people, and should be trained as a long-distance operator, which was a nice step up the ladder for someone as new as I was.

After I had been in Windsor about six months, my nephew Leonard moved away and I had to find somewhere else to live. By then I was making reasonably good money at Bell, and had accumulated some savings. I wasn't at all extravagant. I didn't spend any money on silk stockings as a lot of the other girls did, and I would buy yard goods and make my own clothes. My mother had taught me well. So when Leonard left I was able to move into a nice girls' hostel, run by a group of well-to-do local ladies.

And it was there that I had one of those fortunate experiences that sometimes shape a person's life. One of the lady directors on the board, Mrs. Rodd, was the wife of a prominent Windsor lawyer, J.H. Rodd, who was in partnership with a Colonel Wigle, who later became mayor of Windsor. Mrs. Rodd took a shine to me and asked me to go and work in her house as a maid.

At first, I didn't want to accept. Being a maid seemed quite a comedown from being a long-distance operator at Bell. My sister Sadie had finally got tired of working on the farm and at the hotel, and had run away from home and followed me to Windsor. I tried to persuade Mrs. Rodd to take Sadie instead of me. I told her that Sadie could do much heavier work than I could. (I really was just a wee slip of a girl. I doubt that I weighed even 80 pounds at that time.) But Mrs. Rodd wouldn't hear of taking Sadie. She wanted me. She promised my duties wouldn't be too hard. She had a cook and other staff for the heavy work, and all I would have to do would be the pastry and some light upstairs work and laundry.

Then, when she told me how much she would pay me I did some rapid figuring. With my full room and board supplied, I could save enough in a year to pay my way through business college in Windsor. That was it. And so I embarked on my career as a housemaid, still on my way to being a stenographer.

CHAPTER THREE

The Rodds had a beautiful home, the nicest house I had ever been in. Little did I know that years later I would have one like it, in a posh part of Toronto, the city that had so scared me on my way to Windsor. We girls each had our own room on the third floor, and as Mrs. Rodd had promised, my work was not hard. After Windermere, in fact, it was a breeze: a little light cleaning and dusting, doing the laundry in the basement, and making pastry. I wouldn't call myself much of a cook nowadays, but I could make a good pie then. And Mr. Rodd loved them. He took to calling me "my little girl" and "Miss Viola," and I used to feel more like one of the family than a maid, because they were so nice to me.

The Rodds had one daughter, a tall, beautiful blonde named Olivia, who was away at Bishop Strachan School in Toronto. And whenever she came home she would make straight for the kitchen to greet me, and we would chatter away and giggle like sisters. Poor Olivia. She had a tragic life. She was in love with a young lawyer, a big, handsome fellow named Walker Whiteside, and she wanted to marry him. But her parents thought she was too young. She was only about a year older than me, so they took her on a world cruise, hoping it would all blow over. It didn't though, and they had to agree to let her marry.

I remember I was sent to the bank to pick up one of their wedding presents, a cheque for $10,000. That seemed like a million to me in those days, and I was so relieved when I managed to get it back to the Rodds' house safely. It paid for their home and they settled down and had several children. But when he was still very young, Walker had a catastrophic stroke and died. It was a hard, hard time for Olivia, and soon afterwards she had a heart attack, and she, too, died young. It was such a sad story.

After I had been at the Rodds' about three months, the girl who did the heavy work, scrubbing the floors and that sort of thing, heard that her mother had died suddenly, and she had to leave and go home. Mrs. Rodd tried several girls in her place but wasn't satisfied with any of them. And I must admit they were very sloppy. So I volunteered to do the heavy work as well as my own.

At first, Mrs. Rodd wouldn't hear of it. She didn't think I was strong enough. But when I told her about my days scrubbing the floors at Windermere House, she agreed to let me take on the new duties, and gave me a good raise. I didn't get quite the whole amount that the other girl had been making, but the extra money helped my savings build up.

On Saturday mornings, I would go to the market with Mrs. Rodd and on the way home we would stop off at Mr. Rodd's office; everybody worked on Saturdays then. While Mrs. Rodd went into her husband's office to talk to him, I would wait in the outer office. There were nine lawyers in the partnership, and I would sit there watching their nine secretaries at work. Oh, how I envied them. They looked so cool and confident. More than ever, I was determined to be a stenographer.

Finally, when I had been at the Rodds' about a year, I had saved up enough money to pay my way through business college. My mother's youngest sister, Sarah Johns, lived in Walkerville, which had not yet been amalgamated into Windsor. Her husband was an engineer at the Hiram Walker distillery there. And Aunt Sarah agreed that I could go and board with them while I went to the college.

So the day came when I had to tell Mrs. Rodd I was leaving. It was awful. I was in the basement doing the laundry when she came down to get something. And I said, "Mrs. Rodd, can I talk to you?" She wondered what it was all about, but I went on, "I don't want to leave, and you're going to be cross with me, but I'm so anxious to go back to business college, that I must give in my notice."

Well, by that time we were both in tears. Mrs. Rodd didn't want to let me go. Not that she wanted to stand in my way, but she felt protective toward me, and like my own mother, I guess, she was afraid of what might happen to me. But when Mr. Rodd came home that night he told her, "Oh no, you've got to let her go. She's ambitious and she'll do well." They were both wonderful people.

I promised I wouldn't leave until Mrs. Rodd had found a girl to replace me, and suggested that I should write to a friend of mine, Annie, a farm girl from near Barrie. "She can do all the work I can do," I told her, "and she's a better cook than me." So Mrs. Rodd agreed and when Annie arrived she took an immediate liking to her, too. Annie stayed with the Rodds for about three years, until she left to marry my cousin, Elmer Johns.

Elmer, I think, had been kind of sweet on me. But I introduced him to Annie when she arrived, because by then I was going steady with the man I thought I wanted to marry. I met George MacMillan at a dance the night before I went to work for the Rodds, in 1920. He was four years older than me, a big, easy-going fellow with, in those days at least, a thick mop of wavy black hair and kind eyes that twinkled whenever he smiled, which he did a lot. I've met some people whose eyes stayed the same even when their mouths seemed to be smiling, and I must say I never liked them.

George came from northern Ontario. He was born in Killaloe, and when he was about eight or nine his folks took him to Charlton, about halfway between Cobalt and Kirkland Lake. He started work at the age of 14 as a helper in a lumber camp. When the Great War broke out, he was too young to join the services, but he found a job in a munitions plant at Parry Sound. After that he went to Flint, Michigan, and worked in a factory until his family moved down from the north to Windsor, and he moved back in with them, working for the Canadian National's express department.

I took a liking to George the first time I met him, even though he couldn't dance at all. He didn't have any music in him. But my father had told me I wasn't to go with anybody who smoked or drank, and George did both. So after we had been going out for a while we split up. By that time, I had become very fond of his family, particularly his mother, who was a marvellous lady. I would meet her occasionally and we would go over to Detroit, and I'd visit her at home when I was sure George wouldn't be there.

I was going out at that time with another boy, an electrical engineer named Lester Lambert. But eventually I realized it was George I really wanted, and after about three months we got together again, and George gave up cigarettes to please me. Even then, if I smelt liquor on his breath I wouldn't go out with him that night. Oh, I guess I gave him a real hard time, but George was strong enough, and patient enough, to take it without losing any of his manliness.

While I was going to the business college I would go back to the Rodds' from time to time to help Annie if they were having a party. And once, after I'd been in the college for about three months, Mrs. Rodd sent for me. I couldn't understand why, and my first thought was, my God, what have I broken? I was always careful to tell them if anything like that happened.

So I went, and after I had had dinner with Annie in the kitchen, the Rodds invited us to have coffee with them in the library. That's when I realized I wasn't in trouble. Instead, Mr. Rodd said, "How's my little girl?" And we got talking and he wanted to know how I was doing. I said I was getting along fine. And Mr. Rodd said, "Momma and I have been worrying about you. We've been wondering whether you've got enough money, because we'd like to help you."

Well, I was so touched I began to cry. No one had ever offered to help me like that before. But I managed to tell him that I was okay, that I still had enough to see me through the college. So Mr. Rodd said, "Well, dry up your tears, and remember if you ever do need anything we want to help you. We're very proud of you." And when I got up to go, he gave me a hug. He really did treat me like his daughter.

They were so kind, the Rodds, but I was always a very independent girl and I'm glad to say that I never needed to accept their help. I got my certificate from the college about eight or nine months after I had started there, and was lucky enough to get a job right away, over in Detroit.

I'll always remember going to the interview, at a wholesale plumbing and hardware company. My heart sank when I saw that there were about eight girls in line ahead of me, looking very cool and elegant. They were all wearing lipstick and lots of make up, which I didn't use in those days. And they all had smart clothes and silk stockings. I felt very dowdy in my homemade clothes. But I was the one who got the job.

It didn't last very long, though. After I had been there about two weeks, working as a stenographer at last, the boss called me in. I was scared stiff, wondering what I had done wrong. But he told me, "There's a fellow in Windsor who wants me to let you go. He says he needs you in his office." Well, of course, it was Mr. Rodd. Annie had told him about my new job, and I don't know whether he knew the people at the Detroit company or not, but anyway he called them and more or less demanded that they send me to him.

Once again, I was very nervous. I didn't know whether I'd be able to cope with the work in a law office, being so inexperienced. But everyone was very kind to me, and I guess I caught on quickly. At any rate, I made it my business to read every book about the law that I could lay my hands on, and began to learn about deeds and contracts, and a lot of other things that came in useful in my later career. And before very long, I learned what sort of cases each of the nine partners in the office specialized in. So when people came into the office wanting to see a lawyer but not knowing which one would be best, I would find out what their problem was, and be able to take them in to the partner they ought to see. I didn't play my favourites, and Colonel Wigle and Mr. Rodd seemed quite pleased that I was able to direct the traffic, as you might say.

I had not been working in the law office very long, and was still boarding with my Aunt Sarah, when I got the opportunity to buy a house — well, a shack, really. It was more like a two-car garage, at the back of a lot. The price was $1,600 and change, and somehow I managed to scrape together a down payment on it. I was tickled pink to have my own place, be it ever so humble, as the song says. And soon after I bought it, my brother Jim, who was eight years older than me and had been working in the mines up north, found a job in one of the forges in Windsor and moved in with me. So now I was a landlord, at the tender age of 18.

When I had been going out with George about two years, it was the summer of 1922, we decided to schedule our vacations to coincide and go visit my dear sister Lizzie in North Bay. When we got there, we discovered that there was a one-dollar excursion to New Liskeard on the old Temiskaming and Northern Ontario Railway. This was the line Fred La Rose was working on when he found the silver at Cobalt. They call it the Ontario Northland now, but in those days the trains made so many stops as they wound through the north country, and ran into so many delays, that the T. & N.O. was nicknamed the old "Time Is No Object." George had relatives in New Liskeard, and more to the point as far as I was concerned, a girlfriend. So we decided to take the excursion. I didn't know how serious George was about this girl. I found out later that he was engaged to her. But I wanted to see what she was like, and how serious he was about me.

Well, she turned out to be quite a nice girl, but I decided George needed me more than he needed her. One shouldn't speak ill of the dead, but she was not a great one for getting up in the morning, or washing the dishes. I have always been an early riser, and I certainly don't believe in leaving the dishes pile up for a day or two. We didn't discuss that at the time, of course, but George made it obvious that he preferred me to her. So that was an important visit for us.

It was important to me, too, in another way. New Liskeard is one of three small towns that practically merge into each other on the west side of Lake Temiskaming, the others being Haileybury and Cobalt. Cobalt! That was a magic name for me, because of the stories my brother Joe used to tell. And I remembered the name of the mine he worked in. It was the Coniagas, and I was bound and determined I was going to see it. So while George was off visiting his other girlfriend, I persuaded one of his friends to drive me the few miles down to Cobalt.

In those days, with the big silver mines still going strong, Cobalt was a much busier place than it is now. It's a pleasant enough town, but there's hardly a straight stretch of street in it. The original road-builders back at the start of the century had to weave their way around to avoid all the hills and gullies on the town site, and sometimes they even had to make a sharp bend to skirt around mine shafts sunk right in the centre of town.

When we arrived at the mine, we found it was closed that day, because of a holiday. But I managed to locate the man in charge of it, the mine captain, told him about Joe, and asked him to take me down underground. Well, he was horrified! "I can't do that," he said. "We never allow women underground. It's bad luck." That was a widely-held superstition in the mining industry for years, and I read somewhere once that the present Queen Mother, when she was Queen Elizabeth, was the first woman to go underground in a Canadian mine, on one of the royal tours. That was definitely not a true story, because I beat her to it.

I coaxed and coaxed that poor mine captain. "I can look like a boy," I said. "Just give me the right clothes and no one will ever know I'm a girl." I was slim enough to get away with it, and I just worked on him until he gave in and provided me with coveralls and big miner's boots. Then I tucked my hair up under a miner's helmet, and we got into the cage to go down into the dark below. I suppose I should have been scared stiff as the cage began to clatter its way down, but instead I was enthralled. All those stories Joe had told me came back to me as we walked through the empty tunnels and the mine captain pointed out the veins of silver in the rock. It was not at all as I had imagined it, and nothing like the silver you see in a jewellery store. I marvelled at all the hard work the miners had to do to blast the rock from the walls, then haul it away to be crushed and go through all the other processes necessary to extract the silver from it.

It was one of the most glorious experiences of my lifetime, and I was completely hooked on the glamour of mining. All I had heard about big business till then was about Ford and Chrysler and General Motors. I didn't know anything about the Hollinger and the Lake Shore and all the other wonderfully rich mines in the north country. But I came away from that trip determined to learn all I could about mining.

When I began to study it, I learned that the Coniagas mine, which produced almost 34 million ounces of silver before its ore ran out, was one of the first discoveries made at Cobalt, back in 1904. And strangely enough, it was one of two rich mines found on the same day by a Cornish prospector, William G. Trethewey. He called one of them after himself, and he took $600,000 worth of silver out of the Trethewey before he sold it for a million dollars to a group headed by a Toronto stockbroker and grain dealer named Jack Bickell, who would go on to become one of the most powerful mining men in Canada.

The name Coniagas, which was given to Trethewey's other mine, had always puzzled me. What did gas have to do with digging rock out of the earth? But in my reading I discovered that the name was invented by Dr. Willet G. Miller, Ontario's first full-time provincial geologist, who did the pioneer work on the Cobalt silver ores. He named it for the chemical symbols for cobalt (CO), nickel (NI), silver (AG), and arsenic (AS), all of which were found in the rocks at Cobalt. But I still think it was a funny name for a mine! No doubt Trethewey didn't care, because he made more money out of the Coniagas than he did from the Trethewey and set himself up on a model dairy farm at Weston, outside Toronto.

Back home in Windsor after our holiday, George and I began to get really serious, and in the summer of 1923 George went off to Windermere to ask my father for my hand in marriage, as they used to say in the old novels. Well, my dad was tickled pink by that. None of the other boys who had married my sisters had ever bothered to ask for his permission. And he replied, mind you I only have George's word for this, "Well, if you think you can handle her, it's okay with me."

So we were married in October that year. I was only 20 when we took the plunge, but I never regretted it, right up to the time when poor George died, in 1978. It was not a big wedding, but my mother and father came down from Muskoka to Windsor for it, with three of my brothers, and I was glad of that. And thanks to the generosity of one of Mr. Rodd's clients, George and I were able to move into a nice house right away.

Old Matt Dean was a building contractor: a tall, straight-backed man who always wore a high stiff collar and carried a bible. He looked more like a preacher than a contractor, and he used to chew me out if he ever heard me using even a mild cuss-word — not that I did that very often. When the news got around that George and I were going to get married, Matt offered us one of the new houses he was building in Ford City. And to show how generous he was, he took my old shack as the down payment, crediting us with twice what I had paid for it. That left us with a mortgage of just over $7,000, and we were able to make the payments at first with no trouble.

The house was what they used to call an income bungalow, even though it had two storeys. The top floor was, in effect, a separate self-contained apartment as big as the downstairs. So when times got tough later, George and I lived downstairs, and I rented out the upstairs to boarders: single young men who worked in banks and trust company offices nearby. They would pay nine or ten dollars a week, in cash, on Saturday. And every Monday morning I would take this pile of small bills, because eventually I had eight or nine boarders, into my bank to pay into my account.

As time went on, the bank manager began to get worried about where all those small bills were coming from, and he called me into his office and asked for an explanation. He must have been very embarrassed, because he hemmed and hawed a lot before coming to the point. When I finally caught on to what he was driving at, I was furious. I didn't know anything about prostitutes in those days. "I'm not that kind of girl," I snapped at him. And he was a very apologetic man when I told him where the money really came from.

CHAPTER FOUR

A year or two after George and I were married, Matt Dean took me aside in the office one day. He had continued to take an interest in me, and I think he had been watching how I handled the clients when they came in to see one or other of the partners. "You know," he told me, "you shouldn't be behind a desk. You'd do better if you were out meeting the public. How about selling houses for me?"

Well, I didn't know much about the real estate business, except what I had learned from buying my own house, but he said he'd show me the ropes. And so I began to moonlight for him, selling his houses at night and on weekends. Very often, the prospective buyers wouldn't have much money, so perhaps I would find a lot that they could buy and use as the down payment on a house.

Times were good in Windsor in those days. The big Depression hadn't yet arrived. And so I began to make money in addition to my salary. And Colonel Wigle and Mr. Rodd didn't mind my moonlighting, because whenever I made a sale I would channel the business to the firm.

I had a lot of outside activities in those days, because I always liked to keep busy. Early on, I became secretary of the Windsor No. 4 Chapter of the Order of the Eastern Star, a woman's organization something like Rotary, that does a lot of good charitable work. And I was very honoured, when I was only 26 years old, to be chosen as Worthy Matron of the chapter. The work kept me busy many evenings, but it was valuable experience in organizing things and getting people to work together.

I suppose I might have gone on to make my career in the real estate business if George and I had not received what turned out to be a very important letter in 1926. It came from an uncle of George's, a prospector known as "Black Jack" MacMillan. Uncle Jack was a bachelor, and when he wasn't living in the bush, he stayed with George's Aunt Agnes in New Liskeard. In all his years prospecting, he had never struck it rich, and now he was getting old and going blind.

In those days, to keep a mining claim in good standing, prospectors had to put in 40 days of what was called "assessment work" on it every year, clearing the ground, digging trenches, cutting lines, and that sort of thing. Jack had a couple of claims he wanted to hold on to, but he was too sick to do the work that year. And in his letter he offered George a half-interest in them if he would go north and put in the required work.

In his younger days, George had been taken out prospecting by his father and Uncle Jack, and he knew a bit about minerals and how to recognize promising looking ground. I remember him telling me about his first chore on one of those prospecting trips as a boy. Jack had found a little showing of gold on a property east of Kirkland Lake. He pointed it out to George and told him if anyone came along he was to rush and get a pail of water and pour it over the showing to keep it looking good! When Jack's letter arrived, George was out of work. He had been caught in a CNR express lay-off. So we agreed he would accept his uncle's offer, and take my younger brother Ed up north to help him. Ed was about 18 at the time, and he was living with us. A while before this, I had become worried that he and Reg, who was four years younger than him, were not getting a proper education back in Windermere. So I had brought them to Windsor to be with me and go to school. My mother was furious and she came after them to get them back.

Reg was not really mature enough to realize the importance of getting an education, and he went home with her, so I wasn't able to do very much for him, until much later in his life, when he made a very unfortunate marriage. But Ed stayed with me, and he was delighted at the prospect of going into the bush with George. Also, my annual vacation was only a couple of weeks away, and we agreed that I should follow them up north to spend it at their camp.

Jack's claims were in Grenville Township, a bit north and west of Kirkland Lake, and when the time came for me to join George and Ed, they hiked out of the bush to meet me at a little station on the T. & N.O. called Sesekinika, where the train didn't stop unless someone flagged it down. George and Ed had bought some fresh supplies at the general store before my train arrived, and they had their packs on their backs. I had outfitted myself with a pair of riding breeches and high boots and I also had a pack, containing a change of clothes and other odds and ends I thought I might need. So we set off through the bush looking quite professional, with, George told me, about two miles to go.

My train had arrived at Sesekinika late in the afternoon, so the sun was beginning to set as we marched along, and the evening glow exactly matched the glow in my spirits. I'm sure I didn't really expect to find any gold on my holiday, but just being out there in that wilderness was thrill enough. The air was so crisp and clear, and the silence so immense when we paused occasionally for a breather, that I really felt as though I was in another world, and that we were the only human beings who had ever passed that way. As landscape, the rough bush country of northern Ontario is not to everyone's taste, but there is a curious magic to it. And if you once fall under its spell, it stays with you all your life. It certainly has with me.

It was nearly dark when we got near the old shack George and Ed were using as living quarters, and I was startled when George stopped suddenly and said to Ed, "Mmm. It looks as though we've had a visitor." I didn't know what he meant until he pointed out the pail they kept their honey in, lying beside the trail.

And sure enough, when we reached the shack, its one window

was broken, and we could tell by the tufts of hair sticking to the frame that a bear had broken into it. That old shack wouldn't have won any architectural awards in its prime, but now it was a shambles. George had left their supply of food wrapped up in a blanket on the bed, or what served as the bed — a wooden frame covered with spruce boughs — and the bear had ripped the place apart trying to get at whatever food wasn't safely protected by cans. George said later that it had probably got its snout stuck in the honey pail and only managed to free itself when it was heading off down the trail.

I had thought when I left Windsor that I was game for anything. But the idea of a bear bursting in on me while I was asleep was just too much. There was no way, I told George in no uncertain manner, that I was going to stay the night in that shack. Fortunately, George knew that another prospector, Art Wilson, from Sesekinika, had a cabin a couple of miles away from ours. And so we set off in the dark to take refuge with him. Some prospectors carried guns, to shoot rabbits or birds for food. But George, and I later, never would. We didn't relish the idea of shooting anything. But I insisted we take the axe with us. Ed offered to carry it, but I said, "No, I'll take it," though I shudder to think what might have happened if that bear had jumped out at us, and I had tried to beat it off with the axe.

Prospectors are hospitable people, and when we arrived out of the night, Art Wilson and a couple of his buddies who were sharing his cabin gave us a warm welcome, in more than one sense of the word. Those northern nights can be pretty chilly even in the summer, and they had a cheery fire going in an old carbide drum they used as a stove. Art had a couple of dogs, fierce-looking huskies, and I was almost as scared of them as I had been of the bear. But after the commotion caused by our arrival had died down, they stretched out beside the stove and went to sleep.

In no time, the other two prospectors fixed us supper — that old bush stand-by, baked beans — and then they spread out their bedrolls on the floor and offered us visitors the bed. George and Ed turned in right away, but by then I had become enthralled by

Art Wilson's stories and I sat up most of the night listening to him.

Perhaps it was just having a woman to talk to because Art's wife stayed in Sesekinika when he was away in the bush. Or perhaps it was the old pro's delight in showing off his knowledge to a newcomer, but Art told me all sorts of fascinating tales about prospectors.

There was old Harry Preston, for instance, who was trudging through the bush in "the Porcupine," as the area around Timmins is still known, back in 1909. Suddenly, he slipped on a rock and as he struggled to keep his balance his heel scraped away a patch of moss. Harry could hardly believe his eyes. You can very seldom see gold in a rock formation with the naked eye. You usually have to "pan" for it or send the rock away for an assay. But where Harry's boot had scraped away the moss, he saw a vein of what prospectors call "free gold": gold visible in the rock in its natural state. That discovery eventually became the fabulous Dome mine, which went on to produce well over half a billion dollars' worth of gold.

Then there was young Benny Hollinger, who had been a tool-sharpener at the nickel mines in Sudbury before talking a Haileybury bartender into putting up a grubstake of $45 for him, so that he could go prospecting in the Porcupine. Benny, too, found free gold. The property he staked was eventually developed by Noah Timmins, who had made his Cobalt fortune into the giant Hollinger mine.

Of course, not all the early prospectors were as lucky as that, and one of the unluckiest must have been Reuben D'Aigle, who had searched the very ground where Benny made his discovery two years earlier, and had abandoned his claims in disgust. At the time Art Wilson was giving me this informal history lesson, I can hardly believe now that it was more than 60 years ago, one of the biggest success stories of them all was still being written, by an American named Harry Oakes. Harry arrived in Kirkland Lake flat broke in 1911, at around the time the first hints of gold were being discovered in that area. Harry had trained as an engineer and had then gone prospecting all over the world. When he came to Ontario, he made it his business to learn all he could about the geology of the

Kirkland Lake area, using the government mining offices. And gradually he formed a theory that the "main break," the gold-bearing rock structure, passed right underneath the lake that gave the town its name. Everyone ridiculed him, of course, but Harry was a patient man, and he took to examining the files in the mining records office for the district, at Matheson. Then, as claims in the area he wanted came open because some earlier hopeful had given up and stopped doing his assessment work, Harry began to assemble them for himself, in great secrecy.

It took him a couple of years, but finally he was ready to achieve his lifelong ambition, which was to own his very own mine. With money gathered up from his relatives back in Maine, he began to sink a shaft on the south shore of the lake, and then drive a tunnel underneath the water. Several times he almost had to give up because of lack of funds. Often, he had to talk men into working for him in return for shares in his company, rather than wages. But Harry was a fanatic and he persevered when everyone thought he was crazy.

Finally, his theory proved correct and he hit high-grade gold ore under the lake. Within a few years his Lake Shore mine went on to become the richest gold mine of its day in Canada, and Harry became a millionaire many times over. He bought a big estate in England, created another one for himself near Niagara Falls, and in due course he was made a Baronet.

But in later years I always felt sorry for Sir Harry Oakes. His initiative and determination created hundreds of jobs for Canadians and millions of dollars in new wealth for this country. He gave lots of money to charity and to the Liberal Party, which was then in power. He would dearly have loved to be honoured by his adopted land. It would have been so easy to give him a Senate seat or something, but no one ever did, and he eventually turned his back on Canada and took his huge fortune to the Bahamas. I can still remember all the headlines when he was murdered there in 1943, and no one has ever solved that crime to this day.

Harry Oakes was one of the few prospectors successful enough to develop one of his finds into a mine. More typical of the breed was another legendary prospector Art told me about. That was Sandy McIntyre, whose name was originally Alexander Oliphant. He changed it when he fled to Canada from his native Scotland to escape an unhappy marriage. No one knows how Sandy acquired the prospector's skills in his adopted country, but he became one of the best, and, according to Art, one of the most popular. He was a big strong man with a full red beard, and everybody liked him.

Unfortunately, Sandy also had a tremendous liking of his own, and that was for the most famous product of his native land. In the end it prevented him from reaping the benefits of his successful prospecting career. In 1909, he staked the claims that were developed into the McIntyre, one of the "big three" gold mines of the Porcupine. That mine went on to pay out millions of dollars in dividends, but the only connection Sandy ever had with it was that it was given his name.

Long before the money was raised to develop the McIntyre, Sandy had disposed of his claims. In 1910, evidently short of money for his favourite beverage, he sold a quarter-interest in them to a broker for a mere $300. Then he proceeded to sell the rest of his interest in dribs and drabs and it seems he didn't make much more than $5,000 from the land that eventually became worth millions.

Sandy took it all in stride though, and a little while later he was hired to explore a group of claims in Kirkland Lake. Once again, he found gold, and this time his discovery was developed into another rich mine, which became the basis for a huge mining empire: the Teck-Hughes. Sandy received a bonus of 150,000 Teck-Hughes shares for his pains. Those shares eventually rose to more than ten dollars each, but by then, Sandy had long since sold them in one block, for only $4,500.

Art Wilson never made any big strikes like Sandy McIntyre. In fact, very few prospectors ever do. But as Art went on telling his stories — I can still see his cheery chubby face now, lit by the little oil lamp flickering in that cabin — I began to realize what it is that makes men take to prospecting. It is not just the chance of finding a pot of gold at the foot of the rainbow. It is something more than that. The real attraction is the life itself.

Oh sure, all prospectors are optimists by nature. They have to be. And they never stop hoping that one day they will strike it rich. But in the meantime, they revel in the freedom of the prospector's life: the long days out in the open, the bacon and beans or freshly-caught trout frying on the fire beside the lake when the sun has gone down, the scent of the woods, and the eerie cry of the loon.

Above all, prospectors relish being their own masters. They can go where they like, when they like, with no time-clocks to punch or bosses looking over their shoulders. And they have the satisfaction that comes from knowing that if they're going to succeed, it will be by their own efforts. Sure, luck often enters into it, but there are a lot of successful men who will tell you that if you work hard enough you make your own luck.

Anyway, by the time Art was through telling his stories, I had made up my mind that I would learn all there was to know about prospecting, so that one day I could enjoy that life too. As it happened, Art was at a bit of a loose end at that time, and we hired him next morning to help us work on Black Jack's claims. So he became my first tutor.

I'm afraid we never did find anything on those claims, either then or later. But we were able to help Jack in another way. When we arrived at New Liskeard on our way back to Windsor, we found that he needed an operation to prevent him going blind. The only thing was, he couldn't afford the $90 the operation was going to cost. I was the only one in the family with that kind of money, and I gladly gave it to him. I liked old Jack, even if he was a bit of a rascal.

CHAPTER FIVE

When I got back to Windsor, sunburned nose and all, Mr. Rodd must have decided my "holiday" in the open air had done me a lot of good. Dear man that he was, I'm sure he used to look at me, only five feet tall and as thin as a rake, and worry that I was too frail for my own good. He would have been astonished if he could have seen me digging trenches on Black Jack's claims! But anyway, he decided that in future he would give me every July and August off to go up north.

I was delighted, and settled down even happier than before at my work in the law office. But I think that even then I had decided I wouldn't end my days as a stenographer, and was trying to figure out some way of eventually making my career in mining. In the meantime, I realized that the more I could learn about legal matters like deeds and contracts, the better off I would be in the future. The future was any of the mining divisions into which the mineral-bearing areas of the province had been divided. A prospector could also stake six claims for other license-holders, provided he didn't stake more than three for any one individual. So you would often find one or two prospectors working for a group and quite a large area could be tied up that way.

Each claim consisted of an area of 40 acres, which had to be staked just as the authorities required. You had to drive your first post into the ground at the northeast corner of the area you wanted, the second at the southeast corner, and so on. Then you had to nail numbered metal tags to each post and blaze lines between them. The tags were supplied by the government recorder in charge of each mining division, and once you had staked your claim, you had to register it with the recorder within 15 or 30 days, according to how far it was from the records office. There was a registration fee to be paid at that point. This was five dollars for a claim staked by the license-holder himself, and ten for a claim filed on behalf of another license-holder.

Once these legal requirements had been met, the prospector was free to start exploring his claims, and he had the right to anything he found, provided he kept up his annual assessment work. You were supposed to sign an affidavit swearing you had done the required work, because the government obviously couldn't afford to send inspectors all over the bush keeping tabs on every prospector. But this wasn't really a problem, because most prospectors were only too anxious to do their work. After all, the only reason they had staked their claim was in the hope of finding something worthwhile on it. You would only stop doing the work and let your claim lapse if you were convinced there was nothing on it. Of course, there have been lots of cases through the years of valuable discoveries being made on re-staked ground given up by previous prospectors. That is part of the thrill of the game. You never can tell. Mother nature can play some funny tricks on you.

As for the equipment a prospector needed, George and I assembled our stuff gradually. But it didn't cost all that much in those days to equip an expedition for a season in the bush. I still have among my papers a 1934 brochure put out by the Ontario Department of Mines, as a guide to prospectors. This itemized all the equipment, tools, and clothing needed to put two men on the trail as prospectors. With a month's food for both, the total cost was placed at less than $300!

I must say I became quite nostalgic when I came across that

prospector's guide the other day. It said a cotton duck tent large enough for two, seven feet by nine feet, could be had for $15. But it recommended, to save weight, one made of silk, for $84. Nylon, of course, was still way in the future. George and I made do with the cotton duck.

The canoes we used in those days were covered with canvas, painted until it was quite smooth. And we always carried a length of ten-ounce duct tape for patches. The guide said two prospectors could get along with a 16-foot canoe if they carried only limited supplies and stuck to small lakes and rivers. But it recommended bigger ones, 17 to 18 feet, as being safer. A new one, it said, would cost $75, but they could be bought secondhand for $30.

The guide estimated the total cost of tools at $13. The most important, it said, were the axes, which, as long as a man had a supply of matches carefully kept dry in a watertight holder, could save his life by enabling him to build a fire if he was lost. The absolutely essential "grub hoe," used by prospectors to dig trenches, scrape away moss to get a look at the rock beneath it, and chip off samples for analysis, could be had for $1.50.

The list of food supplies suggested for two men for a month provided what was for those days quite a good balanced diet. It was headed by 50 pounds of flour and 40 of bacon and salt pork, and six pounds of dried beans. But it also included three pounds each of dried apples, peaches, prunes, and apricots, and two pounds of raisins, which I guess were valuable sources of vitamins for men so far away from fresh vegetables and fruit.

The list went on and on: Rice, cornmeal, rolled oats, a dozen soup tablets, a dozen OXO cubes. And it suggested quantities of those indispensable ingredients for suppers around the camp fire: two pounds of tea and two pounds of coffee or cocoa. In all, the guide estimated a month's supply of food for two would weigh about 200 pounds and would cost from $25 to $30.

The good folks at the Department of Mines also reminded anyone thinking of becoming a prospector of the need to protect himself against those twin curses of the north, black flies and mosquitoes. Those convenient spray cans of insect repellents now available even in variety stores in the city had not yet been invented, of course. Instead, the guide recommended a "fly oil" consisting of a pint of pine tar, a pint and a half of olive or sweet oil, an ounce of citronella, and half an ounce of carbolic acid. Oh, how that messy stuff used to smell! It was certainly no threat to the cosmetics manufacturers down south, but it was better than being bitten half to death.

There was a lot of useful advice in that little 12-page booklet, though by the time it came out in 1934, George and I considered ourselves veterans of the north. And there is only so much you can learn from the written page, after all. The rest has to come from experience. For instance, it is one thing to read about the tradition of friendly hospitality in the bush country. It can be quite another thing to actually experience it, as I found on one of our early summer trips up north.

George and I were tramping through the bush one day when we came across a shack where an old prospector lived alone, except for about ten mangy-looking mongrel dogs who milled around us in what I thought was a very menacing way. "Don't worry," the prospector told me. "They won't hurt you, they're my family. And great little helpers they are, too," he chortled. "Why, I never have to wash a single dish. I just set 'em out after I've finished eating and these fellers clean 'em up as nice as you please."

Well, after George and the prospector had chatted awhile about the country round about, the prospector remembered the unwritten rule about hospitality and offered us a mug of tea and a plate of beans. I was about to suggest to George that we ought to press on our way, but his warning glance stopped me. The unwritten rule also says that once hospitality is offered, it is bad manners to refuse it. So I swallowed hard and accepted my fate, desperately hoping all the time that I wouldn't get sick. And thank goodness, I didn't.

Another thing I had to learn about life in the bush is that time up there doesn't always mean as much as it meant to me, bent on being an efficient stenographer in a law office in the city. There was the occasion on one of our early trips when I wanted to go in to see a gold showing near Matachewan that had been found by a prospector named Claude Cook. Technically, Claude was my nephew. His father was a widower who had married another of my older sisters, Janie, though I didn't know him all that well.

Matachewan was already known as a gold-producing area, and when I heard that Claude had this showing, I was naturally interested to see it. The nearest point to his claim that we could reach by road was Elk Lake, which is about 40 miles northwest of New Liskeard. From there we would have to travel about six miles north on the Montreal River.

George and I arrived at the landing at Elk Lake early on a Sunday morning and managed to find a local Indian who said he would take us to Claude's claim for six dollars. I handed over the money and he said he would go off to buy gasoline for the outboard motor he had on his canoe.

Well, we waited around that landing for a couple of hours, and finally I went into a little general store nearby to ask if they knew this fellow and whether we could expect him back. The man behind the counter said, "You didn't give him any money, did you?" When I said I had, the man said, "Well, don't expect him back until he's spent it at the bootlegger's." And sure enough, it was afternoon when our boatman showed up and he was fairly prancing. "Let's go," he said, reeling all over the place. "Let's go." I was furious and told him, "I'm not going anywhere with you in that state." And I made him swear that he'd take us next day, which he did, even though I think with his hangover he'd have rather stayed in bed.

Claude was quite excited as he pointed out his gold showing to us when we arrived, but neither of us thought it looked too promising, and in fact it never did come to anything. Nor did George and I find anything worthwhile on those early trips, but we worked hard and learned a lot about prospecting.

Nowadays, people exploring for mines have access to all sorts of "high-tech" tools, from Geiger counters to scintillometers and a host of other instruments so complicated I can't begin to understand them. Some measure the earth's gravity, others the electrical conductivity of various rocks. That sort of thing. But when George and I started out, prospectors had to rely on their eyes, their grubhoes, and whatever practical knowledge of geology they could pick up along the way.

One thing you always looked for was an "anomaly": some feature of the landscape that looked different from the surrounding countryside. This could be a place where two different types of rock overlapped. Valuable minerals were often deposited in fissures between layers of different rocks when they were being formed all those hundreds of millions of years ago. Quartz, which the old miners called "white rock," often occurs between two layers of different rocks, and sometimes it contains gold. Or your anomaly could be a place where the leaves of the poplars were yellow instead of green, and you might poke around trying to discover if there was some interesting mineral in the ground causing the change in colour. We also used to look for "gossans," or patches of stained rock. A reddish stain, for instance, could indicate the presence of copper. Or it could be worthless iron sulphide. And a pinkish stain might indicate the presence of silver.

Once a prospector has found a rock formation that he thinks looks interesting, the next step is to chip off a piece for closer examination. If you have an experienced eye, you might be able to tell what you have found with the pocket magnifying glass all prospectors carry. Or, if you find a rust-coloured oxidized vein running through the rock you may think it contains traces of gold, in which case you might try "panning" it.

A gold pan is like a frying pan with no handle. To use it, you first pulverize some of the oxidized material — a mortar and pestle being part of the well-outfitted prospector's equipment — and then swirl it around in water. Gradually, the heavier material will sink to the bottom, and you occasionally tilt the pan to empty out the lighter stuff. Finally, you end up with a layer of sludge in the pan, and if you are lucky you might be able to see specks of gold in it.

Sometimes, to get a worthwhile sample, a prospector might have to blast the rock with dynamite. At first, George didn't want me to try my hand at blasting, but once again my experience on the farm came to my rescue. My father and I had used dynamite to clear stumps from our fields.

The final test to discover what you have found is, of course, a proper assay by experts. In my day, for every claim you filed with the mining recorder, you received a couple of coupons entitling you to two free assays at the government laboratory in Toronto. The suspense while you waited for the assay results could be unbearable. However excited you were, the results more often than not were disappointing. The mineral you thought you had found might just not be there. Or it might be there but in such small quantities that it was not worth trying to mine.

Occasionally, though, and this is what keeps prospectors going, your assay might indicate that you have ore in commercial quantities. In my day, for instance, an excellent result would be one that indicated ten dollars' worth of gold to a ton of rock. But even such a thrilling result as that does not mean you have found a mine. There are a lot of other stages to go through before you can say that, as I shall explain later.

CHAPTER SIX

In the closing years of the 1920s, as we all headed toward the tragedy of the Great Depression without realizing it, I began to feel more and more unsettled. I was torn between my desire to take a gamble and get into the mining business somehow, and my reasonably secure life in Windsor. Matt Dean evidently sensed my restlessness, because he offered to help me set up my own real estate business.

I had been quite successful selling houses for him, but I hesitated awhile before deciding to take the plunge, because I hated the idea of turning my back on Mr. Rodd after all his kindnesses to me. But as usual, Mr. Rodd encouraged me in what I wanted to do. When I told him about it, he congratulated me and wished me well in my new career. And he told all the partners in the law firm that if I didn't make a go of it and needed to find a job again, they were to take me back, no questions asked.

It soon turned out that I had chosen a bad time to go out on my own. Even before the stock market crash in the fall of 1929, it was getting pretty hard to make a buck in Windsor, and my new business didn't exactly prosper. Finally, Neil Black, one of my boarders who made his living selling Christmas cards for a Toronto company, suggested that George and I could do better for ourselves if we moved to London. George had been out of work for a long time and had nothing to lose, and when Neil persuaded his boss to let me sell wholesale cards for him in the London area, I decided to pick up stakes and move.

We held on to our house in Windsor. I had a lady move in to look after the boarders, and we rented a big house in London for I think it was $90 a month. Again, I took in a few boarders to pay the rent and coal bills, and tried to establish a real estate business to supplement the money I made selling the cards.

But it was now 1930, and the Depression was really beginning to bite hard everywhere. I finally decided I would be better off spending the summer months in the bush, prospecting full-time, and selling Christmas cards and real estate for the rest of the year.

Up till then, George and I had managed to finance our summer trips to the north by ourselves. But staying in the field for the whole season was obviously going to cost much more money, and by now I had learned enough about the mining business to know that a lot of prospectors were financed by what they called "syndicates."

Syndicates were very important in the development of the mining industry. They were a stage short of a properly-constituted limited company, but they had to meet certain legal requirements and they gave small investors, gamblers if you like, a chance to band together in the hope of striking it rich.

A group of people would buy "units," for say ten dollars each, and the money they subscribed would finance the prospectors while they staked claims and explored them. If a mine resulted from the efforts made on their behalf, the investors would exchange their units for shares in the company that developed it. In addition to having what amounted to wages paid by the syndicate, the prospectors would be given perhaps a third of the units free as their share of the adventure.

On one of our trips up north, George and I had staked some claims in Bowman Township, west of Matheson, a station on the T. & N.O. to the northwest of Kirkland Lake. This was gold country, and we had high hopes for our claims. So I decided to try to finance a full season's exploration up there by forming what I called the Bowman-Matheson Gold Syndicate.

But first I had to get a statement certifying that I was financially responsible and had sufficient assets to meet the legal requirements for establishing the syndicate. So I went to one of the leading auditing firms in London, Foote and Rafuse. George Foote, one of the partners, was a hail-fellow well-met type, who loved his golf, and he welcomed me into his office. Of course, living in London, he was not at all conversant with the way things are done in the mining business. But he listened to me politely enough as I explained my plans, until he discovered how little money I had. Then it suddenly seemed he was too busy to take on any more business. But his partner who shared the office with him, a tall, slim, quiet-spoken man named Les Rafuse, said, "Wait a minute, George. I like the look of this little girl and her plan seems sound enough to me. I think I'll go and see what I can do for her."

So we walked over to my house; it was quite near his office, and he began to question me about my assets. Well, there was the equity in my house, a little furniture, an old Model T Jalopy we owned by now, and my bank account, which didn't amount to much in those days. All in all, Mr. Rafuse had quite a job to make it all add up to the $2,000 I needed for my certificate. But somehow he managed it and I set out to round up enough friends and contacts to buy my ten-dollar units and put me in business.

Mr. Rafuse was a very nice man and we became good friends. I can't say the same about George Foote. Quite a few years later, when my personal account with the firm had probably reached about half a million dollars, Foote invited me to lunch and as we chatted he said, "You remember, Viola, that time you first came in to see me, and I said I was too busy to handle your affairs?" I replied, "I sure do." And Foote had the audacity to say, "Well, I'm not so busy now. How about letting me do your books instead of Les Rafuse?" Well, I was never one to use cuss-words, but I just blurted out, "Go to hell!" And Les Rafuse continued to handle my personal financial affairs until he died a few years ago. A younger partner of his, Mr. Ford, then took over.

I forget now how many units I managed to sell in the Bowman-Matheson Gold Syndicate. It wasn't very many, but eventually I accumulated a "grubstake" big enough to finance me for my first full season in the field. By now, George had found a job in a broker's office, after being out of work for ages, and I assumed he would want to stay behind in London. So when I told him what I was going to do, I said I knew enough about the north to be okay by myself, and he could go on with his new job. But George wouldn't hear of it, and gave his notice the next day. So we packed the Jalopy and set off to seek our fortune in the north country.

Soon after we arrived, Art Wilson told me a story that made my blood boil. Through the years we had become very friendly with Art. On one of our early trips, in fact, when we were strapped for funds, we practically lived on onions his wife grew in their garden at Sesekinika. And I still love onions.

Anyway, we were chatting around a campfire one night when Art told me that he and a couple of his friends had been cheated in a deal with some investors from Buffalo, New York. Art and his friends had eight claims in Eby Township, west of Kirkland Lake, and they had found an outcrop of quartz with a small gold showing. The Buffalo group had agreed to pay them to do some more work on the claims, and Art and his friends had been persuaded to put up their land titles as a guarantee that they would do the work. When the work was concluded, the Buffalo investors were supposed to take over the titles for a payment of, I think it was about $7,000. But somehow those Buffalo sharpies had managed to get the claims transferred to them without making the promised payment. With my experience in Mr. Rodd's office, I couldn't believe it. "They can't do that to you, Art," I said. I was really shocked. "Well," said Art, "they've done it."

But I wasn't prepared to let the matter rest there. I decided to drive down to Toronto and take up Art's case before the Mining Court of Ontario, where a wonderful old judge named Tom Godson presided for years and years, settling all sorts of mining disputes.

On the day set for the hearing, I went to court with a lawyer I had hired on Art's behalf, and soon realized he was making a complete hash of things. He kept on missing the point so I decided I had to get a new lawyer. When the hearing ended for the day I made some inquiries and was advised to get in touch with a lawyer named Kelso Roberts.

Before moving to Toronto in 1929, Roberts had practised in Cobalt and Kirkland Lake for several years so he knew all the ins and outs of the mining business. Years later, of course, he went into politics and became attorney-general of Ontario.

It must have been after ten at night by the time I called him to ask him to take over Art's case the next day. His wife answered the phone, and I discovered later that it was a bedside phone and they had turned in for the night. But when I explained the case to Kelso, he agreed to represent Art and told me to meet him early next morning at his office.

I was there, bright and early, and as we walked from his office to the elevator on our way to court, he told me his fee would be $50, and he apparently wanted it there and then, in advance. I told him I'd pay him at the end of the day, and I did, too. I wasn't sure I had that much money in my account, but I knew a storekeeper in Windsor who I was sure would lend me money with my furniture as security. I paid Kelso thousands and thousands of dollars in future years, because he was my lawyer from that day on. I met Judge Godson a long time later and was tickled pink to find that because I had sat and talked with Kelso during the hearing, he thought I was a lawyer.

Kelso won the case for Art, of course, and he and his friends got their claims back. But they never saw any of the Buffalo money, and I'm sorry to say that in the end the claims never amounted to anything. I learned a lot from that experience, and I guess it was the start of what I consider the most important part of my life's work: the help I was able to give to hundreds of prospectors right across the country in later years.

George and I did some work in Eby Township ourselves later, when we couldn't find anything worthwhile on our Bowman claims. In those days, at the start of the "Dirty Thirties," we were all looking for gold, even though some of the richest mines have always been base metal mines. Think of the billions of dollars that have been taken out of the Sudbury nickel mines since the first of them opened in the closing years of Queen Victoria's reign.

But gold mines had a special advantage during the Depression, because as industries stagnated all over the world, the prices brought by other metals slumped to disaster levels. In 1932, for instance, the domestic price of copper in the United States fell to a record low level of five cents a pound, and Washington put a duty of four cents a pound on imported copper. This, of course, was a terrible blow to Canadian copper producers. The international price of nickel also fell drastically, to the extent that several of the Sudbury mines had to close and hundreds of men were added to the ranks of the unemployed.

The price of gold, on the other hand, was fixed by international agreement at $20.67 an ounce and the mines were able to sell all they could produce. In fact, Ontario's gold mines almost doubled the value of their production in the first three years of the Depression, from just over $35 million in 1930 to more than $60 million in 1933. And that was a lot more in those days than it sounds now.

So gold was definitely the thing when George and I started out, and the atmosphere in the north was full of excitement, even though conditions were so terrible in other parts of the country. I have been an enthusiastic reader of the mining industry's bible, *The Northern Miner*, for about 60 years now. And in its first edition for 1933, *The Miner* carried an editorial with the headline "A Great Gold Boom Has Started." Among other things, this editorial said, "Those who believe that gold stocks have gone 'far enough' are advised that they haven't seen anything yet."

That prediction may have been a little premature, but it came true with a vengeance the following year. President Roosevelt, trying to get the U.S. economy moving again, raised the price Washington guaranteed to pay for gold to $35 an ounce.

The new price turned a lot of what had been considered waste rock into ore, in other words, rock that could be mined at a profit.

And new mines were opened on known gold deposits which had so far been left untouched because the cost of mining then would have been more than the gold would have brought at the old price.

So the boom kept on and on all through the '30s, until gold fell on hard times during World War II. The only thing was, George and I were not finding gold, or at least, not enough to be worth mining. So I began to look around for some other way to make money in my chosen career.

I mentioned earlier that even if a prospector has a rich find of ore confirmed by a proper assay, he is still a long way from making a mine. The next stage is a diamond-drilling program to try to outline the extent of the discovery. How thick is the ore-bearing layer of rock, and how far does it extend? How wide is it, and do the ore values indicated by the assay hold up across the whole deposit?

A diamond-drilling program in my day cost thousands of dollars, and today some of them cost millions. And if the results are still encouraging then you have the expense of sinking a shaft, building your head frame, installing your hoist, and assembling all the machinery needed to drive your "drifts," or tunnels, into the underground rock. Then there is the added cost of building a mill to crush the rock and extract the gold or copper or whatever else you have found.

Sometimes, with a smaller operation, you might be able to ship your ore to a custom mill operated by an established organization, if there is one nearby. But in any case, finding the deposit is only the first stage in making a mine. Unlike Harry Oakes, most prospectors at that stage have to find someone else willing to gamble all that extra money in the hope of one day having an operating mine.

Occasionally, if they have what looks like a sure prospect, they can persuade a major established company to take on the job of doing all the later exploratory work and developing the mine; in which case, they sell their claims, either for cash or shares in the development company, or both. If they are good bargainers, they can sometimes even negotiate a royalty interest in the profits made by any mine that results from their discovery.

More often, though, prospectors have to turn to a promoter who either has an existing company or is willing to form one to try to develop the find. These smaller companies, known as "Juniors," have historically played an important role in the mining industry. They raise the money to explore and develop prospectors' discoveries by selling their shares, "penny stocks," to those members of the public who enjoy an occasional gamble.

Gambling has always been considered a sin by some people, but a lot more love to take a flutter in the hope of making a killing. You only have to think of all the millions of dollars gambled these days in government lotteries. The plain fact is that all mining ventures in their early stages are gambles. The prospector gambles his time, his experience, and his hard work. Investors, whether they are knowledgeable insiders or just members of the public, gamble the money needed to turn a discovery into a mine.

Even the major companies going into what looks like a sure thing recognize the fact that it is a gamble by forming joint venture partnerships with other companies to share the risk, and the possible reward. And the fact that "penny stocks" have a bad name in some quarters is not because they are all sold by shady promoters. In my day, there were statistics showing that only one property out of a hundred that reached the drilling stage ever resulted in a mine.

That is the gamble. A prospect may be abandoned because the drilling results fail to justify earlier hopes. Or a fall in metal prices may threaten to make the eventual mine uneconomic. There have even been cases where actual mines have been developed, only to be closed down when the ore hasn't measured up to the earlier expectations. As I said before, you never can tell.

The more I learned about the mining business, the more I realized that the people who owned the companies, because they were able to spread the risk, I suppose, were likely to make more money than the prospectors who made the discoveries. And I began to think about it more and more. After all, I had been reasonably successful selling houses for Matt Dean, and by now I was selling Christmas cards by the thousand in the off season. I knew something about legal matters, and by now I considered myself a pretty knowledgeable prospector. So why couldn't I form companies and sell mining shares? I thought about it for a long time, and the more I thought about it the more I liked the idea. So in 1933 I formed my own company, MacMillan Securities Ltd., and opened my first office in Timmins.

CHAPTER SEVEN

Just because I was now in business, or rather, hoping to build up a business, didn't mean that I was going to give up prospecting. And in 1934, George, his brother Mark, and I were doing some work on the shore of the lake, south of Sesekinika.

At one stage, I had to break off to make a quick trip to Toronto, in connection with a deal I was working on for my company. Driving back north, I picked up a boy of about 18 who was hitchhiking. He was from the south, he told me, and he was heading north in search of adventure. On an impulse I told him I was a prospector and asked him if he'd like to join George and me at our camp for a while. Of course, he was delighted. George was surprised to find we were going to have a guest when he met me with the canoe to take me back to camp, but he made my hitchhiker welcome. The only thing was, the boy hadn't told me he had just come out of hospital after a bout of pneumonia.

All went well for a couple of days, but then we woke up one morning to find it was pouring with rain and very chilly. The rain went on till nightfall, and we just had to sit stewing in the tent beside the lake, trying to keep dry. Next day, a Saturday, the boy was obviously very sick again. I told George we had to get him to a doctor right away.

So we loaded the canoe and paddled about three miles up the lake to where we had left the car. Then we headed for Kirkland Lake, with the poor boy shivering and moaning in the back seat. It was nearly dusk by the time we hit Kirkland Lake, and we drove him straight to the hospital. Then we pulled into a general store nearby, just as it was closing, and I went in to buy some groceries.

I told the proprietor I didn't have much money and asked him if he would take a cheque. "My name is MacMillan," I said. "Oh," the man replied, "I used to know a Mark MacMillan. I went to school with him." I said, "Would you like to see him again?" The man said he sure would, and I said, "Well, he's right outside in the car, with my husband. They're brothers." So the man bolted outside and I could hear him whoop when he saw Mark, though how he recognized him I don't know, because he and George had been in the bush for weeks and both had bushy black beards.

When he came back into the store in great spirits, the proprietor told me, "So you're Mark's sister-in-law. You can buy anything you want to buy." I dashed around the shelves and spent about $20 more than I had intended to, hoping I could beat the cheque to the bank.

Then, when he had closed the store, the man came out to the car and talked to us for a while longer. That turned out to be another of those chance turning points that are sometimes so important in your life. He told us how a farmer in Hislop Township had been ploughing his fields, when he turned up some rocks and found gold in them. That was where Hollinger finally opened the Ross mine. And, the storekeeper went on, that had started a gold rush into the township, which was going on right at that minute.

Hislop Township was the next township east of Bowman, where our claims had so far turned up nothing very interesting. And it didn't take us long to make up our minds. We drove back to Sesekinika, changed into our bush clothes, and we were out in Hislop Township staking before dawn broke next morning.

The next few weeks were pretty hectic. When you have a bunch of prospectors flooding into an area trying to take up ground, they call it a staking bee. We were so successful (we eventually tied up about 2,000 acres in the southwest corner of the township, near

Ramore, a station on the T. & N.O.), that the other prospectors took to calling me "the Queen Bee."

Part of our ground butted onto 12 claims staked by an old prospector named Paul McDermott, and we got to know him quite well. We were pretty excited in August that year when a company named Golden Arrow Mining Co. Ltd. was formed with the intention of developing Paul's claims.

Naturally, George and I decided to go to work on that part of our ground first. There was an old falling-down shed on it which some long-ago farmer had apparently used as a stable. It was in pretty bad shape, but we decided we could camp out in it for a while as we explored our ground. I was cleaning it out one day, when Paul came by.

"That's no job for a lady like you," he said. "You come out of there and come with me." Paul knew that as well as prospecting for myself, I was helping other prospectors to form syndicates and raising money for them. "I want you to look at another property I have," he told me, "and maybe you'll decide to take an option on it."

So I went with him, and I was encouraged enough by what I saw that I later took a geologist in to find out what he thought. His verdict was not encouraging, and I didn't do anything more about it. But many years later, long after poor Paul was dead, the property came into the hands of a veteran exploration man named Meredith Holt, better known as "Dit." Just recently, in the summer of 1988, I was invited up to see the first gold brick poured at what is today the Holt-McDermott mine. If only Paul could have been there. How proud he would have been. But that's the way things sometimes go in mining.

By 1934, when I wasn't in the field with George, I was busy at my office in Timmins, and I was starting to make money with my company, arranging deals for other people and selling share issues for companies trying to get started to develop claims. In fact, I was becoming so successful at this that I decided I needed an operating base in Toronto. Early in 1935 I was fortunate enough to find office space there. It was not much more than a cubbyhole, but it was right on Bay Street, the street that had already become famous as the financial capital of Canadian mining.

One of the first deals I handled from my new premises led within a short time to my first big break. Up in Timmins, where my activities were much better known at that stage than they were in Toronto, I was sought out by a man named William Swallow, a Toronto builder. Swallow and a couple of his friends — James King, a Guelph doctor who was also a member of the Ontario legislature, and William Noble, a schoolteacher — were the majority unit-holders in a gold syndicate named the Porcupine Quartet. Their syndicate had leased the rights to four separate 160-acre parcels of land, each consisting of four claims in Whitney Township, about 15 miles east of Timmins.

All the Quartet properties were what are known as "veterans' lots," because they had been awarded by the Ontario Government to veterans of the Boer War. The province was anxious to encourage the settlement of "New Ontario," as the north was sometimes called then. They gave out hundreds of these free land grants in the early years of this century, in the hope that the veterans would establish farms on them and begin to populate the area. Some of the recipients who made the long journey north to see their land immediately abandoned any hope of farming it. Many did not even bother to go and look.

But the grants were not, as many of the disappointed recipients thought, completely worthless. They carried with them the rights to any minerals found on the lots. So the veterans, or their descendants, were sometimes able to sell them quite profitably when mines began to be developed in the north. The descendants of one veteran named Hendrie were without doubt the luckiest of all. His land stayed in the family until, many years later, it was bought for $27 million because it was part of the ground on which the Texas Gulf Company established Kidd Creek, the largest base metal mine in the world.

One of the four land parcels that made up Quartet, known as the Poulet Vet claims, lay immediately to the west of a property owned by a company named Pamour. Even then, this began showing signs of developing into the rich gold mine it eventually became. And early in April 1935, a Toronto mining engineer named J.H. Cecil Waite, after negotiating with Swallow, took up an option on the Poulet Vet. He agreed to pay the syndicate $2,700 immediately, to cover rental payments due during the term of the option to the leaseholders, two Orillia men named Cavana and Bingham. He also agreed to make a further payment totalling $65,000 in installments, beginning on March 20, 1936 and ending on May 31, 1937. If at that time his exploration of the property justified it, Waite said, a company would be incorporated to develop a mine on it, and the Quartet unit-holders would be rewarded with a cash payment and an allotment of shares in the new company.

I still have that option agreement, bearing the original signatures, and there is nothing in it to indicate that Waite was acting for anyone but himself. But when reports about the deal appeared in *The Northern Miner*, they said he was acting for "other parties." And within a very short time the news was out that he had been representing Noranda, which even then was a power to be reckoned with in the mining industry, though it had not yet become the giant that it is today.

Pamour had been formed by a company named Quebec Gold Mining Corporation, which had entered into an agreement under which Noranda would explore and develop its property. Oliver Hall, a distinguished mining engineer who was at that time Noranda's assistant general manager, had engaged a prominent geologist, Dr. A.M. Bell, to explore the Pamour property. Bell soon concluded that the gold-bearing structure that had already been established as running across the Pamour ground from east to west would probably continue under the Poulet Vet claims.

Swallow and the rest of the Quartet people knew nothing of this, of course. Like any other mining company engaged in exploration, Noranda took good care to keep its information secret until it had the ground it wanted sewn up, but once the option with Waite was signed, Swallow asked me if I could sell some of the syndicate units that had not yet been taken up.

Up until that time, the units had been available for their par value of ten dollars. But in the first advertisement I placed for them in *The Northern Miner* in May, I priced them at $20. By August, with the news of Noranda's involvement getting around, I was able to raise the price to $25, and by January 1936, I was selling them for $35 apiece. As later events would soon show, they were a bargain at that price.

In fact, as soon as Swallow asked me to begin selling the units, I began to pick up some for myself whenever I had some spare cash. After all, quite apart from Noranda's interest in the Poulet Vet claims, the other three Quartet parcels were not far away from the Big Three gold mines of the Porcupine — the Dome, Hollinger, and McIntyre Porcupine. So they too might prove to be valuable.

As I continued to buy as well as sell the units, I even managed to pick up some from Swallow himself, and the leaseholders Cavana and Bingham. Why they would have wanted to sell at that stage I don't know. But perhaps they had another prospect somewhere else they wanted to invest in, or maybe they were still hurting from the Depression, as so many other people were.

So 1935 was a busy and exciting year for me. But it was also a very sad one for George and me. In June, while we were still camping in the old stable and exploring our ground next to the Arrow property in Hislop Township, we heard a man calling to us from the road about 11 o'clock at night. The road did not go all the way into our shack, and the man — it turned out to be a storekeeper from Ramore — didn't want to risk his neck trying to find his way across the rough ground to our place in the dark. But when we answered him, he yelled that he had had a phone call from Windsor and George's mother had been hit by a car and was in hospital.

Of course, we threw a few clothes into a bag and set off right away, driving all through the night. But when we got to Windsor the next day, it was too late; the poor soul died a couple of hours before we arrived. I was just as upset as George. I had become fond of his mother the very first time we met, and while I was in Windsor, so far away from the rest of my own family, his family had taken their place. It was an awful time for both of us.

Not much later that summer, George and I had taken the train from Timmins to Toronto to look into some business deal, the details of which I have long since forgotten. Before we returned to Timmins, we wanted to pick up some things from our house in London. Paul McDermott, our prospector friend from Hislop Township, whose home was in Toronto, kindly lent us his car to make the trip. We had just started back from London in Paul's car when I felt terribly sick. I was hemorrhaging badly, and George turned round and drove me straight back to the city. He carried me into my doctor's office and I was rushed into hospital right away for an operation. Afterwards, the doctors broke the news to me that I would never be able to have a child.

Up till then, I guess I had always been too busy to consider becoming a mother. It's not that I never thought about it, but raising a family always seemed like something George and I could do when we were established. Now, when our financial security seemed to be just around the corner, to be told that our chance of having a family of our own was ended forever, proved to be a terrible blow. I'm sure George was as devastated as I was. But he never allowed it to show. As usual, his only thought was for me. Dear George. He was a great comfort to me, then as always.

And sensibly enough, he decided the best thing to raise me out of my depression was to get back to work. So as soon as I was strong enough to travel, we headed back to Timmins, where we had become quite well known and had made lots of good friends. Among our growing circle there were Baptiste David, who owned the Windsor Hotel where we used to stay, and an insurance broker named Jim Bartleman, who was elected mayor of Timmins that year.

Jim was a very popular man in the north country. He was a New Zealander by birth, who came to Canada in 1907 after working in England for a while. After a couple of years in Cobalt, he moved to the Porcupine in 1910, when the gold mines were just getting started there, and set himself up as a machinery dealer.

Jim used to tell us terrible stories about the tragic bush fire that devastated hundreds of square miles of the country around the Porcupine in the summer of 1911, the year after he arrived there.

The flames wiped out the original settlements of South Porcupine and Pottsville, and destroyed the surface buildings at half a dozen of the new mines. The official death toll was put at 73 people. But Jim and lots of the other old-timers used to say it was probably closer to 200, because there were so many prospectors and settlers spread out through the surrounding country.

Anyway, in the fall of 1935, Baptiste and Jim, with a doctor friend of theirs named Oscar Stahl, took over the Golden Arrow company from its previous owners. They invited George to join the board of directors and appointed me the company's secretary. The previous owners, after doing a lot of surface work, trenching and stripping off some of the overburden, had been encouraged enough to get in a diamond drill. The drill traced a main zone of gold-bearing rock for about 2,600 feet. But then they had apparently run out of money.

To raise funds for some more exploration, Baptiste and Jim and the rest of the board commissioned MacMillan Securities to sell a million Golden Arrow shares at 15 cents each. I managed to sell them all, and could have sold more if they had decided to issue them. And the following year I sold out another offering at 25 cents per share, so the exploration work was able to continue.

Among Jim Bartleman's many interests was a weekly newspaper called the *Timmins Press*. For some reason, he decided to sell it, and a young fellow from North Bay talked him into giving him an option on it. How he managed it I don't know, because he was flat broke at the time. George and I took pity on him once and let him sleep on the floor of our hotel room in his sleeping bag, because he didn't have anywhere else to go.

Anyway, this fellow, his name was Roy Thomson, managed to form some sort of syndicate to back him in his bid for the paper. But he had some gall. He invited Jim to join his syndicate. I don't know whether Jim was more astonished or more furious. "Imagine," he told us, "he's trying to sell me stock in something I already own!" But Roy was like that, and the more we got to know him, the more we enjoyed his sense of humour. He was a very comical fellow, with a huge laugh. And he eventually managed to raise enough money to close his deal with Jim and moved his family to Timmins. I used to see his young son Ken shivering on the street corner selling newspapers.

Roy had very bad eyes. He had to wear glasses so thick they looked like the bottom of a coke bottle, but he could sure read a balance sheet. And once he got on to the knack of how to buy up papers, it was just easy for him. He used to tell us he'd have a title one day, and of course we laughed at him. But sure enough, he ended his days as Lord Thomson of Fleet, and his son Ken — the poor little tyke I always felt so sorry for on that street corner — is now the boss of one of the world's biggest newspaper empires.

But to get back to the business of the Quartet syndicate; as soon as Waite had secured the option on the Poulet Vet property, Noranda moved a diamond drill onto it and began to explore it. The Noranda people naturally didn't tell Swallow or anyone else what they were finding, but only a month later, a report in *The Northern Miner* said the drill had outlined an ore body 600 feet long that, it went on, would "probably average half an ounce gold per ton across widths of eight to ten feet."

As things would turn out, the results of Noranda's exploration were even more encouraging than that. And when the time came for Waite to make the first option payment of $5,000, on March 20, 1936, Noranda had already decided to develop a mine on the property. Waite let it be known that James Y. Murdoch, Noranda's president, was ready to negotiate the final terms of the agreement without waiting until the expiry of the option, more than a year hence.

That was my first meeting with Mr. Murdoch, one of the most powerful men in Canadian mining in his day, and a real gentleman. And I met him because by then I had bought so many Quartet units, including most of Swallow's, that I was now in control of the syndicate. It was also the first big deal I had ever negotiated, and if I had known then how big that mine was going to be, I might have held out for better terms. But Mr. Murdoch treated me very courteously, though I'm willing to bet it was the first time he had ever found himself negotiating a mining deal with a woman. I thought his offer was quite fair. Noranda, after all, was putting up all the money to develop the mine, and even though its initial drilling results had been encouraging, it was still too early to predict how the project would work out.

Anyway, Noranda agreed to pay Cavana and Bingham, the leaseholders, $20,000 each, and give them 67,500 shares of the new mine to be divided between them. The syndicate received $25,000 in cash and 67,500 shares, to be divided on a pro rata basis among the unit-holders.

Within days of our signing the agreement, Noranda incorporated Hallnor Mines Ltd. The first part of the name commemorated the long service to the mining industry of Oliver Hall, and the second, of course, came from the parent Noranda.

The Hallnor mine began milling ore in June 1938, and it produced gold worth more than $2 million in its first ten months of operation. It continued to operate for 33 years, producing gold and silver worth altogether $58 million, and the company paid out almost $25 million in dividends during its lifetime.

For some reason that I can't remember now, though I believe it had something to do with negotiations with the tax people, we were not able to distribute the Hallnor shares to the Quartet unit-holders right away. But with Noranda's cash payment of $25,000 in the treasury, we were able to start exploring the syndicate's other claims.

As I recall it now, there were not many more than a hundred participants in the Quartet syndicate at the end, some of them holding only a few units each. And since I held more units than anyone else, I stood to receive the largest holding of Hallnor shares when we were finally able to distribute them. We did not know then, of course, exactly what the Hallnor shares would be worth when that day eventually came. But for the first time since our marriage, George and I could look forward to the future with some degree of security.

CHAPTER EIGHT

By the spring of 1936, when Noranda exercised its option and it became clear there would soon be a gold mine on the Poulet Vet, more and more of my time was being taken up by the affairs of my company, MacMillan Securities. I now had an office in London, where I worked during the winter months. I had been fortunate right from the start in acquiring the services of Ethel Graham, an excellent bookkeeper with experience in accounting, who ran the Toronto office very efficiently when I wasn't there, and stayed with the company until she retired many years later.

But the work I was doing — arranging all sorts of deals, putting prospectors in touch with investors able to finance them and perhaps develop their claims, setting up syndicates and companies for them — demanded my own presence in Toronto. So much so that George and I decided we ought to set up our home there. We started off by living in the King Edward Hotel, which was a sort of unofficial headquarters for the mining fraternity then and for years afterwards. We were able to rent a suite there for — you'll gasp at the price if you're familiar with present-day hotel rates — a mere $50 a month. Of course, the country had not yet pulled through the Depression, and several floors of the hotel were closed off because there just weren't enough guests to rent the rooms.

Once settled in our suite, we began to look for somewhere permanent to live. I remember one real estate agent took me to see an old stucco farmhouse on 75 acres at the corner of Avenue Road and Wilson. That agent must have had a pretty good crystal ball. He coaxed and coaxed me to buy that property, and promised me that if I did, I would be a millionaire before I was 15 years older. The area around Avenue Road and Wilson was all farmland in those days, but today it is just south of Highway 401, which at that point must be the busiest stretch of expressway in this country. It is all built up. That farm today would be worth many, many millions, and I could have bought it for $12,000!

But it was not far enough out of the city for me. I was still a real country girl. I wanted a place where there was water, a river maybe, and trees and fields. And we finally settled on a farm further out, 150 acres on Sixteen-Mile Creek, off Number Five Highway north of Oakville. That was still real country then, before all the modern development really got going.

One of our neighbours out there was James Y. Murdoch of Noranda fame, and we became quite friendly later on. We had a farm manager, of course, and with his help we were able to build up quite a nice herd of Aberdeen Angus cattle. I used to love to watch the calves frisking about in the fields. And having that farm finally enabled me to help my youngest brother, Reg, the one who would never listen to me when I wanted him to get an education back when I was starting out in Windsor.

Reg had married very young — too young, I always thought. And I believe his wife was only 16 when they married. Anyway, around 1937 he was out of work, and with three young children to support, that was no joke. So I found a little house for them and gave him a job helping around the farm.

But soon after the war broke out, Reg volunteered for the services, even though he was nearly 30 years old by then, and they had had three more children while living on the farm. And I'm sorry to say that once Reg went away, his wife took off with another soldier. It was just terrible, and the Children's Aid had to come in and rescue the kids. I tried to adopt two of them, but they wouldn't let me unless I took them all, and with the way I was constantly travelling, I couldn't do that. But the Children's Aid found a marvellous lady up near Midland who took them in. I gave her a lot of furniture and paid for their upkeep through the Children's Aid, and they used to let me have the kids for holidays sometimes. A couple of the girls are grandmothers now, but we keep in touch.

But before all this happened, when we weren't off in the bush, George and I divided our time between the farm and our suite in the hotel downtown. Eventually though, around the time the war broke out, we realized we needed a firmer base in the city, so I began to look for an apartment.

One day, the old man who had tried to persuade me to buy a little farm up at Avenue Road and Wilson came to take me to look at an apartment. But when he arrived in my office he said, and I remember he used to speak very, very slowly, he said, "You know, Mrs. MacMillan, you don't want an apartment. You should have a house. And I've got a lovely house I can show you. It'll only take you ten minutes."

I was dictating a letter to Miss Graham, so I told her, "I'll finish this when I get back," and went with him. He took me to this beautiful, big brick house on the Oriole Parkway. It's not a long drive from downtown Toronto even in today's traffic, and I didn't wait to get out of his car before I said, "How much?" I could hardly believe my ears when he replied, "Seventy-five hundred dollars." In fact, I found out later that the place had cost $18,000 to build back in 1926. When the agent told me he thought I could have it for $2,000 down, I said I'd take it before I even went inside.

And I never regretted it. It was just a wonderful house and a fantastic place to entertain in. In later years, so many rich and famous people came to my parties that I would have to take out special insurance and hire detectives just to guard the fur coats they left in the room I used as a cloakroom when they arrived.

Those years leading up to World War II were pretty heady ones for me. As my business prospered and I began to make more money, I started to set up companies for myself as well as others. One of the first, which I called Airquests Ltd., was incorporated in

1936. It was a normal mining company, authorized to carry on all the exploration and development activities of any other mining company, but it had a difference: I was also able to get it a federal charter that permitted it to operate an airline.

So for a while, as George and I travelled around examining properties and investigating potential deals, we had our own private airplane. I hired a couple of pilots and gave them a part-interest in the company, but before very long we realized we couldn't justify the expense. The plane spent a lot more time on the ground than it did in the air, and the pilots got tired of cooling their heels while George and I were off in the bush examining prospects. So I bought out the pilots' interest in the company and sold the plane.

We never did find anything worthwhile with Airquests, but I kept the charter, and have it still. Who knows? Maybe somebody will want to buy it one day to take advantage of that charter-airline clause in its constitution.

After I gained control of the Quartet syndicate, Swallow and his friend Dr. King naturally resigned from its board of management, which was the equivalent of the board of directors of a limited company. I asked George to take over as general manager, and appointed two new members to the board: a mining engineer from Queen's University I had met up north, Cecil Fowlie, and my old boarder friend from Windsor, Neil Black. I owed him a favour for getting me into the Christmas-card business a few years earlier. He later sat on the boards of several of my other companies.

Another man I appointed to the Quartet board some time later, George Buchanan, was the manager of the Premier Trust Company, and my friendship with him began in a curious way. It was just before the visit to London on which I had to be rushed into the hospital. I went in to the Premier Trust office in Toronto to get a list of shareholders in one of the companies I was interested in. George received me warmly and we chatted comfortably for a little while, and then, very smoothly, he escorted me out of his office. He had been so nice and polite it was only when I got outside that I realized I had not received the list I had gone in there for. I was really mad so I turned right round and went back in and told him, "Look, I came in here for some information, and I'm entitled to it, and I'm not leaving till I get it." So this time he got out the list of shareholders and I made a note of the information I wanted.

George must have been impressed by the way I stuck to my guns, because about a week later, Paul McDermott went in to his office to try to raise some money for one of his prospects, and George asked him, "Did you ever meet a woman named Viola MacMillan?" Paul said, "Yes, she's a good friend of mine, but she's in hospital in London right now, very sick." And you can imagine my surprise when a beautiful bunch of pink gladioli was delivered to my hospital room with a card saying, "Best wishes for a speedy recovery, George Buchanan."

George's advice was very useful to me through those early years, and he, too, served on the boards of several of my companies. He has been dead for years now, but I never see a bunch of pink gladioli without thinking of him.

Right from the start, I was determined not to let my activities in connection with Quartet and the other deals I worked on for my company interfere with my first love, prospecting. Sometimes, I had to practise a little ingenuity to prevent the two aspects of my life from clashing, but I always managed. For instance, I'll never forget the day the stock certificate came from Noranda for Quartet's shares of the Hallnor mine. George and I were just about to leave for the bush on one of our trips, so for safe-keeping I took a large safety pin and pinned the certificate to my bra. We were away on that trip for weeks, and that certificate was pretty well greased up with fly oil by the time we got back. But it was still good for those shares, all 67,500 of them, and they were very close to my heart in more than one sense.

In 1936, with the formation of a company called Kerr-Addison Gold Mines Ltd., there was a flurry of interest in the country around Larder Lake, near the Quebec border about 50 miles north of Cobalt. There had been quite a gold rush into that area in the early years of the century, but the few mines that came out of it never lived up to the hopes of their sponsors. The Kerr-Addison, though, eventually became one of the most prolific gold producers in this country, and George and I joined a lot of other prospectors in trying to get in on the Larder Lake bonanza.

While we were in that country, I came across a little hill in the bush that somehow reminded me of all my hard work on my father's farm at Windermere. I poked around a bit and the more I looked at that hill, the more I was sure it had the makings of a pretty good gravel pit.

Back in camp that night, I told George what I thought and said we ought to get up before dawn next day and stake a couple of claims around the hill. He just couldn't believe I was serious. Of course, he knew about gold and things like that, but he didn't know anything about gravel. And, he said, there was no way he was getting out of his warm sleeping bag in the middle of the night to go on a wild goose chase after gravel, of all things.

In those early days, we used to employ old Art Wilson to help us on some of our trips, and he was with us this time. So I promised to give Art our old Ford Jalopy, if he would help me to stake those claims. By now, George and I had treated ourselves to a marvellous second-hand Graham Page roadster. I remember I sanded it down and painted it a gorgeous dark red colour, and that was in the days before spray cans.

So Art and I got up before daylight and pegged out my gravel hill. Nothing much happened for a while after that. But the Kerr-Addison mine went into production in 1938, and one day I happened to mention to my lawyer, Kelso Roberts, that I had a couple of claims up there that I was sure contained a huge quantity of gravel.

Gravel was needed by the mines for a process that had been adopted by then of "backfilling" mined-out areas, as a safety measure to prevent dangerous rock collapses. Kelso always knew all about what was going on in the mining business. He told me the McNamara construction people had had a scout out in the Larder Lake area for a couple of seasons, looking for a reliable source of gravel for the Kerr-Addison. They were very interested when I approached them, and in no time flat they had bulldozers at work on my hill, around the clock, scooping out the gravel George had not thought worth leaving his sleeping bag for. I received some welcome royalties from that early-morning staking and I have those claims yet. I never did sell McNamara the mineral rights.

In the fall of 1936, we received a report we had commissioned from a well-known consulting geologist, Lawrence B. Wright. It was for the three groups of claims Quartet had retained after the deal with Noranda on the Poulet Vet. Wright found visible traces of gold on one of the properties, and a well-marked "shear zone" on another — in other words, a break in the rock formation that might or might not hold ore. He recommended a further program of exploration involving more trenching and bulk sampling. We made arrangements to have that work, and perhaps some drilling, done during the 1937 season.

By the spring of 1937, Noranda was reporting very encouraging sampling results from the 600-foot exploratory shaft it had sunk on the Poulet Vet. It was clear that our Quartet units were going to be very valuable when we were finally able to exchange them for the Hallnor shares. We couldn't do that yet, because the lawyers on both sides were still arguing about how much tax the syndicate would have to pay on the Noranda deal.

By then, George and I were comfortable enough to be able to plan the first real holiday we had taken since our marriage. So we decided to take off that fall, and drive clear across the continent to California. We took two weeks to get there, and it was a truly wonderful trip. We did all the usual things tourists did in those days, and have been doing ever since, I guess.

That was long before the days of the Trans-Canada Highway, so we drove most of the way through the United States. I remember when we came to the Grand Canyon. No matter how much you've read about that great split in the earth's surface, nothing can really prepare you for your first actual view of it. It is just beyond words.

While we were drinking in our first view of the canyon, I noticed a fellow who looked like an engineer. He had the high boots and britches, and looked quite at home in that country, even though he was just a tourist, like us. When we got talking, it turned out he *was* an engineer, and when I told him we were in the mining business, we got along famously. I told him we were on our way to California and would like to stay there for a couple of months, but we didn't want to be in a big city. So he recommended that we head south from Los Angeles to a place called Laguna Beach.

We followed his advice. We only stayed one night in Los Angeles, which even in those days was too crowded for our tastes, and we arrived in Laguna Beach early on a Sunday morning. The coast was so pleasant around there that we pressed on a bit further south, and after about a four-mile drive we came to a wonderful little place called Three Arch Bay. Right down by the beach, there was a gate across the road with a group of lovely houses behind it. A man came out to see what we wanted, and I asked him if there was a house we could rent there for two or three months. He said, "Oh no, we don't have anything at all."

But this fellow, too, looked as though he could have been an engineer, so I kept him talking, and mentioned that George and I were in the mining business up in Canada. As soon as I said that, his attitude changed completely. It turned out that he was a geologist, and he had even read about us in the mining press. Well, he couldn't do enough for us then. He took us and showed us a house he had for rent right down by the beach, and then took George shopping for groceries. And within an hour we were having breakfast overlooking the ocean. George had brought back three dozen oranges and he said, "I'm going to eat all the oranges it's possible for a man to eat."

The lady next door was a widow, Mrs. Proctor, with a little boy about five years old, and we became friends. Before the week was out, she had organized a party for us to meet all the neighbours, and you couldn't have asked for a friendlier bunch. We kept in touch with Mrs. Proctor for years, and she visited us in Canada occasionally. And when her "little boy" came to visit me a couple of years ago he was such a giant of a man, I hardly had a chair in the apartment big enough for him.

George just loved California. He talked about calling Miss

Graham and telling her to sell everything we owned, not that that was very much in those days, because he wanted to stay in California for the rest of his life!

I believe that nowadays Californians pride themselves on being "laid back," and I guess that would have been a good description for George. He was a very quiet, easygoing guy, not at all one to push himself forward. I've been told that in later years, when I wasn't in the office, he would kick off his shoes and pad around in his stocking feet, with his jacket and tie over the back of his chair. I can believe that, because I know he didn't like to wear shoes. Even when we were younger, in the bush, and he had to wear high boots like the rest of us, he hated to lace them up. If there was a dusting of snow on the ground, people coming along behind us would say, "Ah, George MacMillan is up ahead." They could see the skiffles in the snow made by his laces as they dragged along behind him.

But even though he seemed so casual, George was one of those quiet men who worried about things, so right from the start of our life together I determined that I would not get him involved in any of my ventures. If I was going to be a businesswoman, I wanted to be the one responsible for carrying the load. Even on small things, like having a new telephone installed, I would have the bill sent to me. The company would always want to put me down as Mrs. George MacMillan, and I can't remember how many hassles I had insisting that things be in my name alone, and that all bills go to Viola MacMillan. And I'm glad I did, so that I never had to worry George.

Even later, when I formed MacMillan Securities and my other companies through the years, I never asked George to come in with me, or even to back a note for me. In fact, I don't think he ever borrowed money from a bank after an unhappy experience he had in the '20s, when we were driving home to Windsor from one of our prospecting trips up north. We reached Chatham early in the afternoon, and I wasn't sure we had enough gas to make it the rest of the way to Windsor. We were broke, as usual, so I pulled in outside a bank, and told George to go in and borrow $5. Well, he came out looking very sad and told me the manager wouldn't trust him for any money. I was furious and I jumped out of the car and went in to see that manager. I told him my husband was a very fine man and he could certainly have lent him such a small sum. I went on and on, told him where I worked in Windsor, and how we had been prospecting for the summer and practically gave him our life stories.

Eventually, the manager apologized and offered to accept my cheque for $100, and even let me date it for the first of the following week, so that I could be sure to have the money in my account when it went through. Poor George. I'm sure he felt very badly about that experience, and perhaps that's why he was always content to leave the business dealings to me in later years. Besides, he wasn't a gambler anyway, and to make a go of it in the mining business you have to be prepared to back your hunches sometimes when a more cautious person would hesitate.

As all good things ultimately do, our wonderful holiday in California came to an end, and George and I drove home before Christmas, in good time to start planning our work for the 1938 season. One of our priorities was to do some more exploratory work on behalf of one of the earliest companies I formed, called Virita Gold Mines Ltd. — a name formed, of course, from my own two Christian names. I can't say I was altogether happy about naming companies after myself, but George thought it was a good idea, and it is sometimes difficult to settle on a name for a new company that somebody else hasn't thought of first. And I must admit that the most successful company I ever formed, which came along a few years later, was named ViolaMac Mines Ltd.

The nucleus of Virita was 11 claims we had staked in Whitney Township, and after doing some surface exploration on them, we were sufficiently encouraged to contemplate getting in a diamond drill to follow up our early investigations. The Virita claims lay between two of the remaining Quartet properties, and we decided it would be a good idea to explore them at the same time, so we proposed an option arrangement to the Quartet unit-holders.

This agreement was ratified at the annual general meeting of

Quartet unit-holders, held in Toronto at the beginning of June. It provided for the immediate payment by Virita of $1,200 to cover rental payments on the Quartet properties, and an undertaking to spend $5,000 on exploring them. The option was to receive 150,000 Virita shares, which would, of course, assure the syndicate members a share of the proceeds of any mine developed on the properties.

Unfortunately, that was not to be. The exploration of the Quartet properties turned up nothing worthwhile and we let the option lapse, at around the same time as the syndicate was finally able to go ahead with the exchange of units for Hallnor shares. We held on to Virita's original 11 claims, where the drill results had encouraged us to sink a 50-foot exploratory shaft. But here again, the experts finally came to the conclusion that the traces of gold that had encouraged us to dig the shaft would never support a mine. So Virita turned out to be another of those countless mining gambles that never pay off, and the company was eventually wound up.

But the Quartet unit-holders had no reason to be disappointed with their lot. When the lawyers for both sides had settled on the syndicate's liability for tax, and the agreed amount had been paid from the treasury, the distribution of Hallnor shares was made in December 1938. Since neither we nor anyone else had found gold in paying quantities on any of its properties other than the Poulet Vet, the syndicate was wound up at the same time. And the fortunate investors found that each of their units could be exchanged for 13.5 Hallnor shares and $5 in cash. At the time, Hallnor shares were being quoted in *The Northern Miner* at $9, so that each unit which could have been bought for $10 three years earlier, was now worth a little over $125.

By the time the Quartet unit-holders received their shares, the Hallnor mine was in full operation. Its mill had opened in July that year, and I remember how thrilled I was when George and I were invited to a huge party thrown by Noranda to celebrate the pouring of the first gold brick. James Y. Murdoch was host that night to a sit-down dinner for 120 guests, held in the cookhouse on the neighbouring Pamour property.

One press report at the time called me the single largest share-holder in the mine, which was a little premature. But no matter; it was true enough six months later, after the Quartet share distribution. Mind you, that didn't justify another headline that called me the "lady boss" of the mine! After all, Noranda owned 94% of the issued stock and bringing in that mine so quickly and efficiently was entirely their achievement.

The only thing I was boss of at that time, apart from my own MacMillan Securities Ltd., was the Golden Arrow Mining Company. With Jim Bartleman's encouragement, I had accumulated enough shares to take control of that company and become its president. In December 1938, I reorganized it, changing its name to Golden Arrow Mines Ltd. The new company was capitalized at three million shares, with a par value of one dollar, and existing shareholders received one new share for each four shares they held in the old company.

George and I started out with high hopes for the new company. Under the old owners, surface exploration and some diamond drilling had outlined a mineralized rock structure about 130 feet long, with an average width of 15 feet. Surface sampling had indicated an average grade of about $7 worth of gold per ton, and we set about making plans to sink an exploratory shaft to investigate what lay beneath the ground.

By this time, the Bowman-Matheson syndicate, which had given George and me our start in full-time prospecting, had become inactive, nothing worthwhile having been found on its ground in Bowman Township. So I proposed a deal to the unit-holders under which they could wind up the syndicate and exchange their units for 100,000 shares in the new Golden Arrow company. The unit-holders voted to accept the deal at a special general meeting in May 1939, and the syndicate was wound up.

That summer, of course, our thoughts were never far away from what was happening across the sea in Europe. Along with everyone else, we hoped and prayed that the gathering storm clouds would somehow disperse rather than break into an unimaginable tragedy. It was a forlorn hope, and at the beginning of

September we learned that the worst had happened: only 21 years after the end of what we had thought in our innocence was the war to end all wars, another one, which would prove to be even more devastating, had begun. And no one's world would ever be the same again.

CHAPTER NINE

With the outbreak of war, young men, and many women, of course, flocked to the Colours, anxious to play their part in defeating Nazi tyranny. George and I were no longer young enough to consider that option, and besides, we figured we could best serve the war effort by serving the business we knew best, prospecting and mining generally.

The vital importance of mining to this country was still not really appreciated by the majority of the public. I gave some figures in a speech I delivered, at my accountant Les Rafuse's request, to a branch of the Gyro Club of which he was president in the early years of the war. "Last year," I said, "mineral production value in Canada was well over half a billion dollars. This is approximately one-tenth the annual national income for the whole of Canada."

I went on to say that mining in Canada was surpassed in production by only agriculture and manufacturing, and both those industries benefited indirectly from mining. For instance, the mining industry generated around $120 million a year in wages, spent more than $100 million on equipment and machinery built in the factories of Toronto and other cities in the south, and on food supplies from Canadian farms. Eighty per cent of all mineral production was exported, and the millions of dollars in new wealth the mines created every year helped to pay for Canada's war purchases in the United States, and they helped pay the interest on the money that Canada owes to foreign countries.

The key message I was trying to get across, and I had to keep coming back to this time and again in subsequent years, was that the health and even the very existence of this vital industry was constantly being threatened by short-sighted government policies, devised by politicians who just didn't understand how the business worked. And the target of those ill-advised policies always seemed to be the poor prospector, or his grubstaker.

One of the most glaring examples of this kind of muddle-headed thinking was an amendment to the federal income tax legislation known as Section 32-B, introduced just before the war. This was too complicated for me to even try to explain it all here, but basically it treated a prospector's equity in his property, in other words, any showing of a valuable mineral he found on his claims, as income rather than as his capital asset. This meant he had to pay tax immediately on any shares he received from a development company in return for the rights to his property. In most cases, since prospectors didn't walk around with large balances in the bank, this meant they were being forced to sell a good portion of their shares, their only equity in their property, to pay their income tax long before the eventual value of those shares was established by the development of a mine. In the worst cases, if the stock market broke, for instance, or metal prices slumped, prospectors or the members of any syndicate they were partnered with, who were subjected to the same tax rules, could not only see their equity wiped out, but be left still owing the government a hefty tax bill.

This legislation threatened to have a disastrous effect on prospecting and therefore, in the long run, on mine development generally. What outsiders so often seem unable to understand, apart from the fact that all mining ventures are gambles in their early stages, is that even an established, producing mine is a wasting asset. Every ton of ore taken out of the ground means a mine is one ton closer to its eventual closure. New discoveries must continually be made if the industry as a whole is not to wither and die. And the people the country relies on for those discoveries are the prospectors.

Fortunately, by this stage of history, the prospectors had an organization able to speak out for them, The Prospectors and Developers Association, and the leaders of the P.D.A. were eventually able to make the government realize the fatal flaws in Section 32-B and it was scrapped. Henceforth, prospectors and early-stage developers were able to pay tax on their money as they earned it, like other people, instead of on their capital assets before they were realized.

It was another piece of ill-considered legislation that had led to the formation of the P.D.A. a few years earlier. The Engineers Bill, introduced to the Ontario legislature in 1932, was a classic example of how politicians, when they don't understand the workings of a business, can do untold damage to one group of people in their attempt to help another different group. The bill was apparently designed to make work for young engineers graduating on to the horrible job market of the Depression. It proposed to prohibit prospectors from reporting to anyone on any mineral finds they had made on their own claims. Instead, they would have had to employ qualified engineers to file detailed reports on the merits of their properties.

Anyone who knew anything at all about prospectors and the lives they led should have known that the last thing they were fit for was to be employers. Most of them didn't even want to be employees, though sometimes they had to work for the big mining companies to earn their grubstakes. And certainly after a season in the bush, they didn't have any money left to hire professionals to tell them what they had found. Besides, if they had any ideas about raising money to develop their claims, they would already have had expert opinions on their finds in the shape of reports from the government assay labs.

Unfortunately, unlike professional engineers, prospectors in those days had no organized voice to represent them. Scattered as they were over hundreds of square miles of bush country, they were seldom even in touch with each other, let alone able to band together to defend themselves against harebrained schemes hatched without their knowledge in offices hundreds of miles away. And strangely enough, it was an engineer, not a prospector, who recognized the threat the Engineers Bill posed to prospectors and therefore, further down the road, to the whole of the mining industry.

In 1932, Walter Segsworth, in his early 50s, was a widely respected mining engineer at the top of his profession. But as a 17-year-old boy he had worked underground in a mine in British Columbia, and even after his skill and enterprise had made him well off, he never lost touch with the ordinary guys at the bottom of the ladder. When he heard of the government's planned Engineers Bill, Segsworth canvassed some of his friends and business associates in Toronto and found that they shared his opposition to it. So he called an informal meeting of about a dozen veteran mining men, including such legendary prospectors and mine-finders as Bob Jowsey, Karl Springer, and Arthur Cockeram. It did not take this group long to agree that the only way to fight the bill was to organize.

They got busy among their friends, and on 1 March, 1932, a group of more than 100 prospectors gathered in the King Edward Hotel and formed what they at first called the Ontario Prospectors Association. This industry voice was eventually able to persuade the government to kill its ridiculous Engineers Bill.

Before that year was out, well aware that the investors — prepared to gamble funds to grubstake them and develop their finds — were their natural allies, the prospectors voted to broaden their membership and renamed their organization The Ontario Prospectors and Developers Association. A few years later, by which time its work had become national in scope, the 'Ontario' was dropped, and members were admitted from all over the country.

George and I joined the association soon after its formation, and always supported its activities, if only from the sidelines. But when the war came along, and we were established in Toronto, we decided we had a responsibility to shoulder a more active role in its affairs.

Some time early in the winter of 1941, a group of about eight or nine of the association's most active members gathered at our house for an informal "bull session," to talk over business that might likely come up at the annual meeting in a few weeks' time. They included several former presidents, including Murdoch Mosher, who, with his brother Alex, made several important finds and spent a lifetime prospecting all over Canada. At that time, it was customary for the president to hold office for only one term, and the group also included the outgoing president, John Byrne. "J.J.," as everyone called him, was a real mining veteran. In fact, he was the third generation of his family to make mining his life. His grandfather had worked in a silver-lead mine in Ireland before immigrating to Canada.

Walter Segsworth was also there. Though he was regarded as the "father" of the association even then, Walter never served as its president, because right from the start he had insisted on the importance of the association's leader being a prospector himself. He was on the executive committee though, and his views always carried great weight.

I'm sure Walter had a heart of gold, but he was a tough egg, and he didn't pull any punches when he was talking among "the boys." Murdoch wanted George to be the next president, and he had suggested his name while I was in the kitchen making up a tray of sandwiches for the group. I walked into the room with the tray just in time to hear Walter saying, "No, we haven't had a real good president yet, and you won't do either George. You're too soft." Well, of course that made me mad and I spoke up. I looked Walter straight in the eye; he was sitting down, of course, and I said, "George will make a very good president. I'll see that he does." With that, the others chimed in and said, "Yeah, let's give George a chance." And the funny thing was, I hadn't known Walter Segsworth very well before that, and I don't think he thought women had any business in mining, but once I faced up to him we got along famously.

So at the annual meeting, George was proposed as the new president for 1941, my name was put forward for secretary-treasurer, and we were both elected without contest.

By that time, I had moved my company into a larger office, at

67 Yonge Street, and sometime later I changed its name to Mac-Millan Prospecting and Development. Under the old name, MacMillan Securities, people had expected me to take on all sorts of deals in businesses that had nothing to do with mining, like any other broker. But I was only interested in mining deals, and of course George and I were still spending a lot of our time in the bush prospecting. So the new name was a more accurate reflection of our activities.

Once George and I took up our new duties, I set aside a corner of my office for the association's files and general use, rent free of course. And Miss Graham agreed to work on the association's business on a voluntary basis, as did Mrs. Doris Drewe, who joined her on my staff at around that time.

I had been very impressed with Doris when I met her as a volunteer canvasser for a tag day in aid of the Women's College Hospital. As a member of the hospital's board of directors, I had been asked to organize the tag day, along with Mrs. Conant, wife of the Ontario attorney-general. We had to have a huge organization. I think we required about 5,000 volunteers before we could get a license for the campaign. There was a lot of work to be done, and Doris just absolutely stood out among the rest. After it was all over — I can't remember how much money we raised but the campaign was a tremendous success — I asked Doris to join my staff. She agreed, and she was a tower of strength to both me and the P.D.A. until her retirement many years later. And I owe her a special debt of gratitude for coming back to help me search all my files and jog my memory as I write this book.

The mining industry in Canada was going through a period of enormous change when George and I took over our P.D.A. duties in 1941. In the early days of the war, Canada had faced a great need for U.S. dollars to buy war supplies of all kinds. Obviously, one way to get them was to increase our gold exports. The federal Minister of Finance, J.L. Ilsley, even said in his 1940 budget speech that it was the gold mine operators' "patriotic obligation" to increase their production "by every means known." And to help in that task, the gold mines were given government priority in the allocation of manpower and supplies. So 1940 was a boom year for gold, with the country's production amounting to more than $125 million.

But just around the time George and I took over at the P.D.A. the U.S. Congress passed the "lend-lease" bill, and the allies' need for hard currency was no longer so urgent. The gold-mining industry soon lost its priority for labour and supplies, and fell on hard times. (I shall have more to say about this in a later chapter.) The emphasis now switched to the production of base metals to fill wartime needs.

Side by side with this change, there had been a dramatic slump in the amount of prospecting going on in the country's mining areas. We at the P.D.A. were not the only ones worried by this. In the address to the Gyro Club I mentioned earlier, I quoted a speech that the federal Minister of Mines, Thomas Crerar, had recently made, in which he had said: "Our ore reserves are being drawn upon to a much larger extent than they are being replaced by new discoveries. Unless such discoveries are made, we must, in a few years, face a declining mineral production." I also quoted from the recently published annual report of Noranda Mines, in which the consulting engineer Oliver Hall, who had given his name to the Hallnor mine, had said: "We continued our search for new mines, but found that prospecting had practically ceased. It is urgent that this be revived."

There were several reasons why there were no longer so many prospectors out roaming the bush. A lot of the younger men had joined the hundreds of workers from the mines who had volunteered for military service. But this was only a minor part of the problem. Even those too old to serve, and the investors who might have grubstaked them and developed their finds, had been scared off by legislation such as Section 32-B, and other well-meaning, but ill-advised attempts to wrap up their activities in all sorts of red tape. To bring about the revival of prospecting that Oliver Hall and others were calling for consequently became our priority at the association. But in a lighter vein, as the time for our 1942 annual convention approached, I was asked by the executive committee to organize a suitable commemoration for our tenth anniversary.

Up to that time, the association's annual meetings could hardly have been called conventions. They had been brief half-day affairs, during which the members sat around, had an informal discussion of topics of current concern, elected their president for the coming year, and then broke up. There were no organized technical sessions, only the occasional guest speaker, and no social functions other than those members who were staying in the hotel pouring each other drinks in their rooms. I decided to correct what I saw as these defects.

I organized a full day's program for the 1942 session, with a couple of prominent speakers, and alerted the press so that their remarks would attract some publicity. The main speaker, as I thought was very appropriate, was G.C. "Slim" Monture. Slim was a mining engineer who had gone into the government service and been appointed executive assistant to the wartime Metals Controller George Bateman, another mining engineer with wide experience. I was confident Mr. Monture could explain the government's policy on strategic metals to our members, who at that time still had no formal notification of it. And thanks to my work with Mrs. Conant on the Women's College Hospital board, I was able to secure as another speaker her husband Gordon, the Ontario attorney-general who would shortly serve a brief term as the province's premier. I knew our members were always interested to hear about any legislation or regulations that might affect their activities.

On the social side, I determined that for the first time, women would be made as welcome as men at the meeting, and would be represented at the head table. I even issued invitations to women whose husbands were away in the bush to turn up and take part in the festivities. And I planned a four-course banquet to end the day, with a huge cake to celebrate the association's tenth birthday.

Once my arrangements were all made, I rounded up sponsors to finance the printing of a proper program for the day's events — another departure from custom. The association at that time had no budget at all, since it charged no dues. I may not have made myself very popular by doing it, but I announced at the meeting that henceforth there would be a one-dollar annual fee for membership. That didn't bring in much money at first, because at that time there were only 73 signed-up members. But as word of the association's work began to spread among the prospecting and developing fraternity, new members began to join up in very satisfactory numbers. We had grown to about 600 by the end of that year.

The day's proceedings went off very well, and 150 members and guests enjoyed the banquet and the dance that followed it. There was one big embarrassment however. Three of the chairs at the head table, which should have been occupied by veteran members of the association, remained unoccupied throughout. These gentlemen boycotted the whole event because they objected to the presence of women.

As convenor of the proceedings, it fell to me to make the first ceremonial cut in the birthday cake. Without saying anything to anyone, I also took three generous slices out of it and had one of the King Edward Hotel waitresses wrap them up for me. And next morning I called on all three of the absentees in their offices, and presented them each with their slice of cake.

I won't mention their names in deference to their memories, because their attitude was not all that unusual in those days, and because each of them apologized to me profusely. Ever afterwards they gave me their full support. No doubt by the time I got there, they had heard from their friends what a success the tenth anniversary party had been, and were regretting that they had not been there.

CHAPTER TEN

That tenth anniversary meeting of the association in 1942 was more than just a social success. It also marked the first stage in the revival of prospecting, which everyone said was necessary but no one yet seemed to have done much about.

For a start, we were able to announce, at one of the business sessions, that the federal government had decided to permit individuals and members of recognized mining syndicates to deduct from their income taxes a portion of any money they spent exploring for strategic minerals. This was welcome news, and in fact the scheme proved so successful that it was expanded the following year to apply to mining companies as well.

The association had been lobbying for some incentive such as this, and as its secretary I had made the first of many wartime trips to Ottawa to make our views known to the government. I was courteously received by the ministers concerned, Mr. Crerar, the Mines Minister, Mr. Ilsley, the Finance Minister, and Mr. C.D. Howe. His title at that time, I believe, was Minister of Munitions and Supply, though he was such a dynamic man, and was given so many emergency powers during the war, that he became known, at least behind his back, as the "minister of everything." On this occasion at any rate, our association had no cause to complain about red tape, because the tax amendment we had pushed for was rushed through within just a few days of my visit to Ottawa.

There were several other important fruits of that tenth anniversary meeting, and some of them, I'm sure, resulted from Slim Monture's appearance as one of our guest speakers. I use his nickname because everyone always did. He was very popular and widely admired in mining circles. In later years, we were addressed by many government ministers and officials, and our members looked forward to learning something of benefit from their speeches. But I always felt their attendance at our conventions was pretty well a two-way street. In their informal contacts with our members, before and after their speeches, and in the question periods that sometimes followed, our guests must have been able to sense those matters which were of genuine concern to us.

At any rate, I'm sure this was the case with Slim Monture. I believe he must have taken back to Ottawa with him a concern of his own about one of the things that worried us in those days, and which was partly responsible for the slump in prospecting: the virtually complete absence of any reliable information filtering down to us about the government's needs and policies in the field of mineral resources.

C.D. Howe was the minister responsible for transforming Canada from its peacetime economy into what became known as "the arsenal of democracy." Because of our tremendous production of ships, planes, tanks, guns, and ammunition, Howe had been given very sweeping powers over all aspects of business and industry. To carry out his grand design, he had reached into the business world for "dollar-a-year men," so-called because their companies picked up their salaries as a patriotic duty, to serve as controllers over the various different segments of the economy. George Bateman, the man Howe appointed as Metals Controller, was a mining engineer with wide contacts in the industry. The men he chose to fill the positions on his War Metals Advisory Committee represented all branches of that industry, except for those essential spark plugs, the prospectors and developers.

I'm sure that what Slim Monture, Bateman's right-hand man,

learned at our meeting helped to bring about the change made in that policy later in the year. But the situation early in 1942 was simple. Prospectors and developers had no opportunity to assist the government in the formulation of its metals policies, and no effective guidance as to what role they themselves could play in the country's war effort.

Everyone realized that the emphasis in the mining industry was being switched from gold to base metals. There was a new need for so-called "strategic" minerals, either because of ships transporting supplies being torpedoed or traditional sources of supply falling into the hands of the enemy. But prospectors had no very clear idea about what those strategic minerals were, how to recognize them, which of them were most urgently needed, and how they could best go about finding them. And for their part, with so many wartime controls being imposed, investors did not know what ground rules they would have to follow if they were asked to develop any prospector's finds. It was a very confusing situation.

Slim Monture had called his speech to our meeting "The Battle of the Metals." From it we learned that serious shortages existed on the allied side in a wide range of minerals that included tin, tungsten, mica, copper, manganese, vanadium, chromium, and molybdenum. Some of those metals, like copper, were of course already being produced in Canada by existing established mines. Deposits of others were known to exist, but in the past they had been considered unimportant or impossible to produce at the prices they were fetching before the war gave them a new importance.

Discussing Monture's speech afterwards, the association's executive committee agreed that if anyone was going to find new deposits of minerals known to exist here, or discover hitherto undetected minerals required in the war effort, it would have to be our members. But first they had to be educated in what they should look for.

So off I went to Ottawa again to see what I could do to get the ball rolling. Having been well received by Mr. Crerar previously, I called on him first. For years, I told him, prospectors had been out looking for gold. If they were to find some of the strategic minerals the country now needed, they would have to have some guidance. Perhaps the government's own geologists were the best people to give them that guidance, and could he help?

Mr. Crerar passed me on to William Timm, federal Director of Mines, and I repeated my story to him. He in turn handed me over to Dr. George Young, chief geologist of the Geological Survey of Canada. Though privately I heard later, Mr. Timm had some serious reservations about the reception I would get. Dr. Young had a reputation for being rather blunt and abrasive, and totally bound up in the affairs of his department; it was still early in the year and both he and his geologists were extremely busy preparing for their coming season in the field.

I can remember that meeting in Dr. Young's office as if it were yesterday. It was late in March, and like most steam-heated offices in those days, his was very stuffy. I was shown to a big, old horsehair chair that must have been part of the furniture since the early days of the department. Skirts were being worn rather short in those days, and the prickly horsehair kept scratching the back of my legs. It was so hot, I took off my hat and tossed it into another chair some distance away.

I don't now whether it was that, or the way I kept pressing my case, but Dr. Young seemed very wary of me at first. I repeated what I had told Mr. Crerar and Mr. Timm and said only Dr. Young's excellent geologists could explain to my prospectors what the various strategic minerals were, which ones the war effort needed most urgently, and which geological structures were most likely to contain them.

Eventually, Dr. Young seemed about to agree with my suggestion that the P.D.A. would organize meetings of prospectors if he would provide geologists to give them lectures on the strategic minerals. He asked me whether I could round up 15 prospectors for a class in Toronto. "Oh," I replied, delightedly, "I could have 150 at least." Dr. Young then asked, "How soon would you want my men?" In reply, I pointed out of the window to where there was a maple tree in early spring bud. "Right now," I said, "before those buds are in full leaf. You're a good field geologist, and you know as well as I do that you work best before the bush is in full leaf and the flies are out."

This apparently assured Dr. Young that I could be taken seriously, and he picked up his phone and told his secretary, "Send in Ambrose, Jolliffe, Wilson, Bostock, and Rice." These were his top geologists, all with Ph.D.s in their science and many years of field experience. After they had trooped in, bringing their own chairs, Dr. Young explained my proposal. In no time his men were enthusiastically discussing their arrangements for going to Toronto.

Things moved very quickly after that. I immediately let our members within reach of Toronto know about the scheduled classes, and the Ontario Department of Mines agreed to supply some lecturers to beef up our program. And as soon as word of our plans reached the north country, the prospectors up there clamoured to be let in on the classes and it was arranged to repeat the Toronto program immediately afterwards at Kirkland Lake.

The three days of classes began in the Royal York Hotel in Toronto, on 9 April, 1942. As I had promised, there were at least 150 prospectors there to hear the various lecturers explain how to recognize the most urgently needed strategic minerals, and where they might be found. And after a day off for travelling, the lecturers repeated their three-day program at the Park Lane Hotel in Kirkland Lake. By that time, prospectors in the Sudbury area had heard about the popularity of the lectures, and were demanding the opportunity to hear them, so the program was repeated for their benefit.

Those classes were so successful that within days, by actual government count, in Ontario alone, 600 prospectors fanned out into the bush seeking strategic minerals. But then came a classic example of the left hand not knowing what the right was doing. The Department of Mines and Resources (by supplying us with instructors at such short notice, all of whom could explain the technicalities of their science in terms non-scientists could understand) had rekindled enthusiasm in the prospectors' breasts. Now came an order from the Metal Controller's department that plunged them back into uncertainty. That order was only one of the many that turned out to be necessary. In the interest of the war effort, these powers allowed the Metals Controller to exercise virtually total control over all aspects of the mining industry. And it was certainly not designed, as became clear later, to scare off prospectors. But by a strict reading of the way it was reported in the press, a prospector who came across a possible new source of tin or tungsten, say, and promptly put a pick into it to investigate it further, would technically expose himself to immediate prosecution.

Clearly, if the momentum imparted to prospecting by the government classes was not to be lost, something had to be done to prevent a repetition of this kind of confusion. And shortly afterwards, George Bateman acted by appointing three representatives of the Prospectors and Developers Association to his War Metals Advisory Committee. Two of the appointees were well-known prospectors and mining engineers Bob Bryce and Charlie Houston, and the third was yours truly. I was absolutely delighted by the appointment, not only because it was an opportunity to serve my country in a field I knew something about, but also because it would enable me to keep our members informed about government policies and requirements. Also, by putting forward the prospectors' and developers' viewpoint, I hoped to be able to prevent some of the crossed wires that had hindered their activities in the early days of the war. I realized that most of the confusion had been the result more of a lack of understanding than any wish to be obstructive.

The committee held regular meetings, sometimes in Ottawa, but more often in Toronto. We dealt with all aspects of the government's control over mineral exploration and production, and considered properties all over the country that the government might put money into to ensure production of the required minerals.

As my special responsibility, I was asked to manage the production of high-quality chrome and mica from two small but rich deposits in Quebec. As far as I know, that chrome deposit was the only one known in Canada at that time, but its exploitation had not been economically feasible until the wartime emergency forced the government to take a hand. I supervised the sinking of an inclined shaft down to the ore, which was needed in the production of toughened steel. Everything was very hush-hush, of course, and we didn't even know where to ship the ore until we had a car load ready, whereupon the government would give us our instructions as to its destination.

George, too, had been anxious to "do his bit" for the war effort, as the popular phrase of the day put it. When he volunteered his services to the government, he was directed to help with munitions production. But looking back on those years, I think the most valuable service we rendered to our country, certainly in its long-term effects, was the work we did for the Prospectors and Developers Association.

The response to the 1942 prospectors' classes in Ontario had been so good that we organized an expanded series of lectures right across the country for 1943, once again with the enthusiastic co-operation of George Young and his federal geologists, now supplemented by some of their counterparts in those provinces that had substantial mining interests.

That series began with two days of classes in Toronto in early February, timed to coincide with the annual meeting of the P.D.A. I managed to secure Edward T. Dickinson, executive director of the planning division of the U.S. War Production Board, as one of the guest speakers. From Toronto we crossed the country to Vancouver for two more days of lectures, and then headed back with stops at Edmonton, Winnipeg, Flin Flon, Port Arthur, Haileybury, and Timmins. Our final three stops, where the prospectors were just as enthusiastic about the classes as they were everywhere else, were at Noranda, Bourlamaque, and Montreal in Quebec.

In all, the program lasted a month and a half. George went along to chair the sessions, and I was on hand to supervise arrangements for hotel accommodation and deal with the media. By now I was becoming quite accustomed to speaking on the radio. The classes also gave me a golden opportunity to meet more prospectors, and recruit them to our organization. I took along a good supply of membership blanks and several of those cards containing pins used by dressmakers. Whenever I could persuade a prospector to sign up for membership, I would pin his dollar bill to his application. I had quite a sheaf of papers to hand over to Doris when we finally arrived home in Toronto.

In 1944, we organized another nationwide series of classes, with Sault Ste. Marie, Geraldton, and Kirkland Lake added to the list of 11 stops made the year before.

As a testimony to the success of our program, in the summer of 1944 there was one of the greatest staking and early-stage development booms ever seen in this country. But even before that, prospectors had been making a valuable contribution to the war effort.

Before the war, magnesium oxide was not produced in this country. All our supplies came from Greece. With that source cut off by the German U-boats, and since magnesium was high on the government's list of strategic minerals, Bob Jowsey, one of the P.D.A.'s charter members and our president for 1934, tackled the problem. Bob was a veteran prospector and he soon found a source of magnesium in dolomite deposits in Renfrew County, almost on Ottawa's doorstep.

He then enlisted the services of Dr. Lloyd M. Pidgeon, a brilliant chemist, who was at that time with the National Research Council. Dr. Pidgeon developed a revolutionary process for the production of high-quality magnesium from dolomite ore, while Bob and his associates operated their Dominion Magnesium Ltd. plant at cost for the duration of the war, as their contribution to the national effort. Their Renfrew County plant turned out 20 million pounds of badly-needed magnesium before the end of the war — enough to supply all of Canada's needs, with some left over for our allies.

Other useful wartime finds included mica near Mattawa, Ontario, and molybdenite in Quebec. With the help of ultraviolet lamps, scheelite (a source of the tungsten used in high-quality toughened steel) was identified in many deposits of other minerals where its presence had hitherto been unsuspected, including some operating gold mines.

As the time approached for the association's annual meeting early in 1944, our membership had grown to almost 1,700. So many members signified their intention of attending the meeting that our traditional home, the King Edward Hotel, was no longer big enough to house us. So we moved the convention to the Royal York, which has been the scene of every annual meeting from that day to this.

The Royal York manager I was dealing with when I was making the arrangements knew nothing about our association. And when he heard how many members were expected to attend our convention, he naturally wanted some sort of guarantee that all the bills would be paid. He only became more nervous when I explained our lack of funds, but suggested I could easily get a guarantee from one of the big mining companies.

That offended my independent streak no end. So I talked the matter over with George, and we decided to put up our own personal life insurance policies as security for any convention debts. I also threw in a diamond ring I had acquired in settlement of a debt, which I had had valued at $500 even in those days. This satisfied the manager, but all the convention's bills were paid on time as George and I had been confident they would be, and the hotel never had need to seize our personal assets!

When George had come to the end of his first year in office, the association established a precedent by re-electing him, first in 1942 and then in 1943. Now, George having announced his intention of standing down, the association broke with tradition again. With no dissenting voices, the members elected me to replace him as their president.

The prospectors' choice of a woman to lead them attracted quite a lot of attention in the press, but it didn't surprise me. They appreciated the work I had done for them, of course, but even more than that, they knew I was one of them.

Not all organizations were so open-minded at that time, though. Later that same year, several of the men urged me to apply for membership in the Canadian Institute of Mining and Metallurgy. I received a letter back from its president in Montreal, in which he said that he had thought when he received my application that the institute's membership was restricted by its constitution to men. "However," the letter went on, "to obtain an authoritative opinion, I submitted the matter to Council in session here on December 14th last. They were unanimous in ruling that such was the case."

Charlie Houston, who served with me on the War Metals Advisory Committee, and several other P.D.A. members were so angry that for a while it looked as though they would resign from the C.I.M.M. in protest. I managed to persuade them it didn't matter enough to me for them to take such a drastic step. But Miss Graham and Doris Drewe were also mad — so mad that they had the president's letter framed and hung up in our office, and they wouldn't take it down even when I asked them to.

It was 1954, and I had been president of the P.D.A. for ten years, before the C.I.M.M. changed its mind and admitted me to membership. But in 1978 I received notification that in view of my "long service to the Institute and the Mineral Industry" it had been decided, unanimously again, to designate me as a Life Member. How times change!

CHAPTER
ELEVEN

Whenever we could spare the time from our wartime duties and our work for the Prospectors and Developers Association, George and I continued to take off into the bush prospecting. We did quite a lot of work in northwestern Quebec during the war years, some of it near Noranda, some north of there in Destor Township, and some further east around Val d'Or. We formed a little company we called Macfort, to hold a group of claims we thought looked promising near Noranda. They didn't work out, though, and we surrendered the charter, which wasn't difficult because we never had sold any shares to the public.

While our Quebec experiences proved disappointing, George made a very encouraging gold discovery in the late summer of 1941 in Hislop Township, not far from our Golden Arrow property. The first grab samples he took from a quartz vein about five to six feet wide showed values ranging up to $35 a ton. The find attracted some attention in the mining press, and two established companies tried to buy the claims from us. But we decided to keep them for further investigation.

At that time, we were still receiving good reports from the work on the Golden Arrow property, and we decided to deepen the exploratory shaft that had been sunk to a depth of about 50 feet a couple of years earlier. Then, however, gold mines lost their government priority for manpower and materials and we had to postpone our plans.

It wasn't until early in 1945 that we were able to go ahead again, and we began a program of diamond-drilling that soon detected a new vein on the property. By this time, the Golden Arrow company had more than 400 shareholders, and we decided to apply for a listing on the Toronto Stock Exchange. We still had more than a million unissued shares in the treasury, so there was ample leeway for the raising of more development funds. We finally were able to go ahead with the deepening of the shaft and the construction of a new sleeping camp, cookhouse, and road. These were completed by the early summer of 1946. I believe at that time we had about 40 men working on the property.

By then, Dr. J. Willis Ambrose, one of the first government lecturers at the strategic minerals classes I had organized for the P.D.A., had left the Geological Survey and gone into business as a consultant. An Albertan, Dr. Ambrose had studied first at the University of Alberta, and then gone on to earn his geological degree at Stanford University in California, before taking his Ph.D. at Yale.

He was a fine geologist and I frequently commissioned him to do work for me. In fact, we hit it off from the very first time I met him in Dr. Young's office. At the beginning of 1946 we joined forces to form a company called Variometer Surveys, which did geophysical work for my companies, and on contract for others.

Dr. Ambrose's reports on the ore samples from the Golden Arrow were very favourable during 1946 and we pressed the work ahead as fast as we could. By November, the shaft was down 250 feet and we had started to drive into the rock laterally along the vein. The reports were still good and we pushed the shaft down even further and started another cross-cut at the 400-foot level. In 1947, when these results began to come in, they were even better than at the first level.

But by now the whole gold industry was in desperate straits. The cost-price squeeze that the gold mines found themselves in started during the war when they lost their priority for labour and materials. The situation got worse in the post-war years. First of all, there was the price they had to pay for the skilled labour they needed. During the Depression years, when any man who had a job at all counted himself well off, wages hardly moved upward at all. This changed as competition for the available manpower increased during the war years, and labour costs just skyrocketed as the post-war inflation took hold.

Side by side with this, the gold mines found themselves faced with steadily increasing costs for all the materials and supplies they needed. But unlike other industries faced with that same situation, they were unable to offset their rising costs by increasing the price they charged for their output. In fact, they were actually receiving less for their product after the war than they had been when it broke out.

This was, as I explained earlier, because the price of gold was fixed by international agreement at the equivalent of $35 U.S. per ounce. In 1940, Ottawa pegged the value of the Canadian dollar at 90 cents U.S., and the effect of this was to raise the price Canadian mines received for their output to $38.50 per ounce in our currency. But later the value of the Canadian dollar began to edge upward, until it was selling at a premium above the U.S. dollar. And every time the dollar went up, the price Canadian producers received for their gold went down.

Early in 1947, by which time many gold mines had already closed down, it was obvious that the future of the industry was seriously threatened. Low returns endangered the existence of whole towns that depended on gold, from Yellowknife in the west, through Timmins and Kirkland Lake in Ontario, to Val d'Or and Bourlamaque in Quebec.

The plight of the gold industry was therefore a national problem, and it was clearly up to the federal government to do something about it. After all, it was Canada's membership in the International Monetary Fund and other organizations that forced the mines to sell their gold at the fixed price. The various mining organizations were lining up with advice for the federal government, and I decided I ought to do something about it myself, on behalf of the Prospectors and Developers Association.

I had seen how the gold mines boomed when President Roosevelt increased the gold price during the Depression, and it seemed to me that the logical place to begin my lobbying was in Washington. So I bought a new five-dollar dress, a nice hat, and a pair of white gloves, and headed south. I never did care much for white gloves but everyone wore them on formal occasions in those days.

After making some inquiries, I decided to take my case to the Senate Committee on Minerals. I found out that its chairman was Senator George Malone, of Nevada, which is, of course, a mining state, and I presented myself at his office. The girl who greeted me there was a bit snooty. She said the senator wasn't in, and in any case he wouldn't be able to see me because he had a meeting of the committee as soon as he came back. I think he was out having lunch.

Anyway, I was just leaving when Senator Malone walked in. He was supposed to have quite an eye for the ladies, and he certainly couldn't have been more charming with me. He asked if I had come to see him, and when I replied that I had and told him who I was, he invited me into his office right away. And when I had explained my case to him, he said I should put it to his committee, whose members were just beginning to arrive for their meeting. There were about five of them, I think. I can't remember all their names, but one was Senator Claude Pepper, who represented Florida, I believe. He died only recently and I used to love to watch him on television. He was a great battler for "seniors" in his later years.

The members of the committee listened to me quite seriously as I explained the Canadian gold mines' problems, but they pointed out that they were already under great pressure from their own gold and silver lobbyists from the western states and had so far been unable to do anything about their local problems.

So there didn't seem to be much that the committee could do for me, or the Canadian mines. But Senator Malone suggested that before I went home, I should see some of the financial leaders in New York City. And there and then, in my presence, he telephoned

David Rockefeller, the banker, and Robert C. Stanley, president of Inco, and they agreed to take me to lunch next day.

As a result of that visit to Washington, George and I became quite friendly with Senator Malone and his wife, and they stayed with us in Toronto several times. I was also able to persuade the senator to be a guest speaker at one of our P.D.A. conventions.

Mr. Rockefeller and Mr. Stanley were very sympathetic and helpful when we had our lunch in New York, but they pointed out to me that there were great international difficulties in tampering with the global price of gold, which was at that time, of course, the underpinning for the currencies of the major world nations. However, they added that there was nothing to stop individual countries from assisting their nationals directly through some type of production premium or bonus system, or tax incentive arrangement.

This advice pointed me directly to Ottawa, so a couple of days after I returned home I went there and talked with Douglas Abbott, the federal Minister of Finance, and his deputy, Dr. Clifford Clark. They admitted that I was not the first to suggest what would in effect be a subsidy for the gold mines. They said they were under great pressure from the Canadian Metal Mining Association and various major mining companies. The problem, as the minister saw it, was that no bill proposing assistance to the gold mining industry, which the public was inclined to see as a bunch of fat cats, could survive parliamentary opposition, led by the then CCF party. He was not even sure, he said, that the backbenchers of his own party would support it.

So I then tracked down M.J. Coldwell, the CCF leader, and explained the gold industry's predicament all over again. Mr. Coldwell asked several questions that made me think he was sympathetic to my cause, but eventually he said it would be impossible for his party to support a subsidy for gold production. I tried again to explain the true situation to him, and pointed out that if the industry collapsed it would not only be the shareholders in the mining companies who would suffer. Thousands of workers and their families would be affected as towns like Timmins and Kirkland Lake closed down. It could cost the government far more to take care of them, and perhaps have to pay the expenses of resettling them down south, than it would cost to pay some sort of premium to help the mines stay in business.

With this, Mr. Coldwell became very thoughtful, and said he would discuss the matter with his colleagues. He was about to go out west for a short visit, but said that if I would get in touch with him again in two weeks he would let me know his decision.

As soon as those two weeks passed I went to Ottawa again and contacted Mr. Coldwell's office. The girl there confirmed that he was back in Ottawa but said he was not in his office, so I went looking for him. I found him in the Members' public dining room, sitting by himself waiting to be served, and I walked over to him and asked, "Remember me?" He replied, "Indeed I do. Please sit down." That was very nice, but he then shattered my hopes. "I have unhappy news for you," he said. "My colleagues and I cannot support the kind of gold assistance bill your association advocates."

I was crushed, but the "wheeler-dealer" part of me wouldn't give up, and I persisted. "Even if you couldn't support it," I asked, "would you necessarily oppose it?" I could hardly believe my ears when Mr. Coldwell said slowly, as if he was thinking aloud, "We would not oppose it."

I clasped one of his hands and gasped out my thanks and then sprang to my feet and raced to Mr. Abbott's office with my news. Mr. Abbott said he and his cabinet colleagues would take my conversation with Mr. Coldwell into account when they next considered the position of the gold mines. In the meantime, he encouraged me to lobby all the government backbenchers I could possibly reach.

In all, I spent about two months in Ottawa, pushing for some sort of help for the gold-mining industry. And in November that year I received a telephone message suggesting that I might like to be present in the public gallery of the House of Commons during the afternoon a couple of days later. I was there, of course, and experienced one of the greatest thrills of my entire service to the Prospectors and Developers Association: Mr. Abbott announced that the government proposed to pay a subsidy of $7 an ounce to all gold producers in Canada.

Unfortunately, there were lots of protests at this, and I guess the one that counted most with the government was one from the International Monetary Fund, objecting to Canada's unilateral tampering with the internationally-agreed price of gold. The subsidy plan was quickly shelved, but Ottawa then exhibited some fancy footwork and replaced it in 1948 with what Mr. Abbott described in the House as a "cost plus bonus plan," otherwise known as the Emergency Gold Mining Assistance Act, or EGMA. To get around the international objections, EGMA was a complicated system designed to make up some of the gap between the internationally set price of gold and the actual cost of producing it. It was not, Mr. Abbott said, a subsidy to keep up dividend rates, but was "specifically designed to keep high-cost gold producers, and the communities which they support, alive."

Not all mines benefited from the EGMA scheme. Those whose ore was rich enough to be produced at a cost low enough to assure a profit even at the fixed price did not qualify for any government assistance. But the scheme undoubtedly prevented many less fortunate mines from going out of business before their time, with untold hardship to the communities that depended on them. It went on operating until 1976, at an average annual cost to the treasury of less than $11 million. By that year, no mine was applying for its assistance, thanks to the increase in the price of gold after it was freed from international restrictions in 1968, and left to find its own market level, like any other commodity.

All in all, EGMA was a great success, and I am still proud to have played some part in bringing it about. Unfortunately, it came too late to salvage our hopes for the Golden Arrow property. Perhaps even EGMA could not have made the Arrow into a successful mine at that time. At today's international price of gold, who knows? But more of that later.

Back in 1947, the trouble was that the results of all the exploratory work we had done on the property could only be described as tantalizing. We had sunk at least 65 diamond-drill holes before we deepened the shaft, and Dr. Ambrose reported that they revealed five separate and distinct gold-bearing zones. By the spring of 1947, we had also completed hundreds of feet of drilling underground.

But the results were inconsistent. In one place, I remember, a rock sample assayed out at more than five ounces of gold to the ton, which is very rich. In another place, just about a foot away, the assay showed only half an ounce to the ton. And when we put all the figures together, we decided the average over the whole property was unlikely to amount to as much as one ounce of gold to the ton. This was nowhere near rich enough, at the cost-price relationship prevailing in those days, to make the Golden Arrow into a mine. So in the fall of 1947, even though it was a great wrench after all those years of striving and hoping, we closed down all operations at the site.

That was not the end of the Golden Arrow company, however, for by that time we had embarked on a totally new venture, half a continent away. Like generations of pioneers before us, George and I had heeded the call of the west.

CHAPTER
TWELVE

The prospect that drew George and me to the west was not gold, but a much different metal. We hoped to find lead, and the silver which is often found with it.

The mountainous area around Slocan Lake, in the southern interior of British Columbia, was the scene of a tremendous mining boom during the closing years of the 19th century. The centre of all the activity was the city of Sandon, about ten miles east of the lake. In 1900, Sandon was a prosperous place with about 2,000 residents and it was known as "the Silver City of the Slocan." Today, with most of the lead-silver mines that supported it long since abandoned, it is a ghost town. Only a few restored buildings, one of them converted into a museum to preserve some of the old mining equipment, remain behind to remind the visitor of Sandon's past glory. I first heard about the Slocan early in 1947, from an old friend and extremely successful prospector, Arthur Cockshutt. Back in the early 1930s, when George and I were just starting out in the bush, Art and his partner, Fred MacLeod, had staked some claims in the Little Long Lac area, in the rugged country around Beardmore and Geraldton, north of Lake Superior. Later, with some promotional help from a marvellous old mining man named Joe Errington, they were able to develop these into their own mine.

The MacLeod-Cockshutt operated for 30 years or more, and produced at least $50 million worth of gold.

Now Art had gone further afield, and had somehow secured an option on the Slocan Rambler, an old mine which had lain idle since 1925. In its heyday, the Rambler was one of the largest and best-known mines in the whole Slocan area. It operated for about 30 years, and produced almost 22 million pounds of lead, more than three million ounces of silver, and, in its later stages, close to four million pounds of zinc.

When Art told me about the Rambler and suggested I acquire an interest in it, I asked Dr. Ambrose to go out and take a look at it. He came back quite enthusiastic. The mine, he reported, was one of the deepest in the Slocan country. It was on a steep mountainside, and consisted of 13 levels, reached by four adits, or entrances from the surface. His report said it was well worth further investigation for three main reasons: first of all, the previous owners all those years ago had taken their production from a series of rich but narrow veins in a type of rock called porphyry, but they had apparently not bothered to carry out any lateral exploration that might have discovered parallel structures; secondly, Dr. Ambrose located a new "plug" of porphyry, which the previous owners seemed to have overlooked; and thirdly, he discovered veins of silver-bearing quartz on the surface.

When I received this report, we had not yet decided to close down Golden Arrow's Hislop Township property. But the depressed state of the gold-mining industry had already suggested to us that it would be a good thing for the company to diversify into some other metal. So I incorporated a Golden Arrow subsidiary, B.C. Slocan-Rambler Mines (1947) Ltd., under the laws of British Columbia. Art Cockshutt and his wife, Marguerita, each received 300,000 shares in the new company in return for the option, and Golden Arrow received something like half a million shares. I undertook to purchase 200,000 shares at ten cents, to put some money immediately in the treasury and get the ball rolling. I took options on a further 800,000 shares at prices varying from ten cents to 50 cents, to be exercised at intervals over the following two years, which I was confident I could sell to provide sufficient funds to rehabilitate the old workings. George and I headed on west to begin that task in July of 1947.

Our first job, of course, was to hire a crew to work for us. The "Swedes," we were assured by the locals, were the best workmen. I never did find out whether that term really applied to men from Sweden, whether it applied to all immigrants from Scandinavia, or even all immigrants from anywhere. At any rate, the men we hired were an excellent bunch.

The first stage in reactivating an abandoned mine is known as "de-watering." When they are not being worked, and the pumps that normally operate around the clock are dismantled and taken away, all mines tend to fill up with water, either dripping down from the surface every time it rains, or seeping in from underground sources. The Rambler had been standing idle for almost a quarter of a century, but the de-watering process did not prove to be much of a problem because of the natural drainage provided by the mine's position on the mountainside.

Then we had to clean out the old shafts, and replace the rotting wooden ladders connecting the different levels. When all that was done, and the old camp buildings on the surface were cleaned out and renovated, we were able to start diamond-drilling and have the geologists begin their investigation underground.

As soon as we got the old camp house in shape again, the men lived there during the week. George and I used to drive them home on Friday night to New Denver, the nearest town, near the north end of the lake, and then drive them back again at four o'clock on Sunday afternoon. In those days, you could only get into New Denver from the south; the road has been extended to the north now, but at that time it ran out about three miles from town.

One Sunday afternoon, while we were waiting to pick up the crew, George and I drove up the road a way and I spotted a sign saying "Farm for Sale." I said to George, "Let's take a look at this place." Well, it wasn't really a farm, just a clearing of about an acre in the bush, but there was a nice little house on it with a picture window with a beautiful view right down the lake. The lady living there said she had advertised the place for sale in the Calgary news-papers, for $5,000, and there were supposed to be some people coming in to see it soon. So I made up my mind quickly, once again. I had two $50 bills in my purse and I persuaded her to accept them as a deposit and bought the place on the spot. We didn't have all that much ready cash on hand at that time, but I had a property in Muskoka that some people had been trying to buy from me for several years. I got in touch with them right away. They still wanted to buy, and that deal provided us with our new home in the west.

We had no intention of selling our house in Toronto, of course. I still had my business there and my duties for the P.D.A. But soon after we moved out west I realized I should have a housekeeper to look after the Oriole Parkway house while I was away. And there fate took a hand again.

The Slocan area was one of the places in the interior of B.C. where the government put those poor, unfortunate Japanese people they moved off the west coast when Japan got into the war. And about the time we moved out there, they had begun to release them and the government let it be known that they were available for employment. So I asked the government office in New Denver if they could recommend a Japanese lady who would like a job in Toronto.

They came up with a woman named Mrs. Sumi, whose hus-band had been a gardener in Vancouver before the war. Mr. Sumi wanted to return to Japan now that he was able to, but Mrs. Sumi and her 20-year-old daughter, Hannah, wanted to stay on in Canada. As a reference, Mrs. Sumi gave the name of a geologist in Vancouver. I called him and he was delighted to have news of her. She had worked for him for 20 years, he said, and I could trust her completely. "She's a wonderful person," he told me.

And that's exactly how I found her, and she was with me for 17 years. I had really only bargained for one woman, but Mrs. Sumi refused to be parted from Hannah, so I arranged passage for them both to Toronto. I gave them the keys to my house, plus some cash to get there by taxi from the station and buy groceries and things like that. So off they went.

They had been living in an awful shack in New Denver and Mrs. Sumi told me later she couldn't believe her eyes when she saw my house. I had told them they could have the top floor, which consisted of three bedrooms and a bathroom, all furnished, and they were just delighted. I didn't see them again for about two months, and when I did get home, Mrs. Sumi had washed all the walls in the kitchen and had the whole house shining like a new pin.

I became very fond of Hannah and put her through business college, and she came to work for my company as a junior. But she had a tragic life. Someone, I suppose it was her father, arranged for her to marry a Japanese boy she had never even met. It was all done by mail. I think it was probably a dodge just to get him into Canada. But when he arrived, Hannah insisted on having a legal wedding here. George and I both attended, and were very happy for her. But after a few days, that boy came to me in my living room. He could only speak a few words of English, and he said, "I no like Hannah. I go home." I was furious, and so sad for Hannah.

As if that was not bad enough, some years later I discovered that she had had a lump in one of her breasts for many years. I insisted that she go to see a doctor right away. But it was too late. The cancer had spread all through her body and it wasn't long before she died, still a young woman.

Hannah's misfortunes were years away in the future, of course, when George and I first went to live in New Denver. Among the new friends we made out there was a charming old Englishman named Ernest Doney. For about 19 years, Mr. Doney, as I always called him since he was that type of fellow, had been single-handedly working an old lead-silver mine, the Victor, on another mountain across Carpenter Creek from the Rambler. He lived with his wife, a pleasant little English lady, in a cabin heated by a wood stove, where he used to sit listening to hockey games on the radio. He was friends with everyone; he even used to talk to the squirrels.

The Victor, which began producing in 1923, had originally been owned by a friend of Mr. Doney. When he died, he left it to his daughter, Mrs. Robinson, who was living at that time in Tacoma, in the state of Washington, and Mr. Doney was operating it on a lease from her. Working underground all by himself, with his dynamite and pick and shovel, he would take out little wee lumps of lead, enough to make him about $5,000 a year.

Early in 1948, Mr. Doney, who was getting on in years, suggested to me that I ought to buy the Victor. The property, he explained, also included two other inactive mines, the Lone Bachelor, which had been worked from 1905 to 1923, and the Cinderella, which had closed in 1924 after operating for 20 years. The owner, Mr. Doney said, was prepared to sell the whole property for $50,000, and he would assign his lease to us for a further $15,000.

George and I talked over this offer for some time and decided it would be a good investment for a company we had formed three years earlier, but which had been pretty well marking time ever since. ViolaMac Mines Ltd. was incorporated under the Ontario Companies Act in 1945, with the idea of developing the promising Hislop Township claims George had staked early in the war. We had managed to raise a few thousand dollars for more exploratory work by selling shares, at prices varying from two to 30 cents. But we realized, even before the state of the gold industry forced us to suspend work on the Golden Arrow property, that there was no chance of going ahead with the development at that time. The Victor mine therefore looked like an opportunity to put ViolaMac into business, even if not the business we had originally envisaged for it. So we decided to buy it, and I headed east to raise the money for it.

The owner wanted an immediate payment of $25,000, and was prepared to wait a year for the other half of her $50,000. But if we were to go to work on the property right away we would also have to pay Mr. Doney his $15,000 immediately to buy him out. So I needed to find $40,000, and that was a lot of money back in 1948.

I raised some of it by selling ViolaMac shares at ten cents each, and raided my own bank balance for the rest, or almost all the rest. When the time came to head back to New Denver, I was still $1,000 short of the $40,000 I needed.

I arrived in Calgary with a few hours to wait for the little plane that used to take us into New Denver in those days, so I headed for the Palliser Hotel to have lunch. And here fate took a hand once again. As I hesitated at the entrance to the dining room waiting to be seated, I was hailed by a man sitting alone at a table. He jumped to his feet and beckoned me over to join him. I recognized him at once, of course. It was an old friend, Henry Jackman, who had gone on to the Harvard Business School after taking his law degree at Osgoode Hall in Toronto before he had really made his mark in the financial world. He was a director of I don't know how many companies, and was in Calgary for a board meeting of, I think it was, the Burns meat-packing company.

Anyway, over lunch he wanted to know what I was doing and I told him I was on my way to option another mining property but I was still $1,000 short of the money I needed. "Oh, I'll give you that," he said, reaching into his jacket pocket for his cheque book. "No, no," I said, "you don't need to do that." I was confident I could raise the extra thousand on my house in New Denver.

But Mr. Jackman persisted. "No. Forget about it," he said. "It's just a donation to you. I admire you and what you've done a lot." Well, I couldn't accept a gift, just like that. So I told him I would give him 10,000 shares in ViolaMac in return for his "donation." He didn't want to accept them at first, but I insisted. I pulled out my little notebook and he told me whose names he wanted the shares in. He took 2,000 for himself, 4,000 to be divided between his wife and his mother, and 1,000 for each of his four children, one of whom is a well-known financier himself today, Hal Jackman.

I told him I'd have my office send him the shares and he laughed and said, "Well, I won't sell them until they reach three dollars." He had to wait awhile before he could do that. It was 1953 before ViolaMac shares topped three dollars on the market. And if he had held onto them a couple of years longer he could have sold them for even more; the market high for ViolaMac shares in 1955 was four dollars. That was because, over the next few years, the Victor mine exceeded even the rosiest hopes we held for it in 1948.

CHAPTER
THIRTEEN

When I got back to New Denver and handed Mr. Doney my cheque for the $40,000, I also assured him that he could have a job at the Victor mine for as long as he wanted one. He was very grateful, and very gracious. "I hope you make a million, Mrs. Mac," he said. He always called me Mrs. Mac. I forget now whether he went himself to Tacoma or did it all by mail, but he soon had the owner's signature on the papers, and by the end of May, 1948, I had set up a subsidiary company, ViolaMac Mines (B.C.) Ltd., to handle all ViolaMac's business in the west. This eventually became quite substantial.

Like the Rambler, the Victor mine was on a mountainside, but until we took it over it had been opened on only five levels. All the previous work on it had been done by hand, but George and I planned to expand and modernize the operation. So our first task was to hire men to clean up all five levels and repair the old tracks used for the carts, which took the ore to the portals of the tunnels.

By now, we were beginning to realize that our hopes of reopening the Rambler were not likely to be justified, so we hired half a dozen or so of our "Swedes" from there to work on the Victor, and George took charge of the operation.

The previous operators at the Victor had used a very basic early method of mining known as "hand-steeling." One man held the bit, which was like a sort of long crowbar, and his mate drove it into the rock with a sledgehammer. Well, that form of mining had gone out of style at about the same time as the horse and buggy began to be replaced by the automobile. We planned to use compressed-air drills, like everyone else. That meant our crew had to install an air compressor and lay a network of hoses for it before we could get down to actually extracting any ore.

I also commissioned Dr. Ambrose to do some geological mapping of the property, as it was cleaned out. I didn't realize it at the time, but that job had never been properly done before. It was only years after George's death that an associate of ours told me a story about the Victor, that George had told him years earlier. It seems that Mr. Doney had once had a friend of his do a survey of the mine in return for a bottle of whiskey. The trouble was that this fellow was a surface surveyor who knew nothing about underground work. And, as George apparently told Mr. Doney, "Ernest, you should always give more than a bottle of booze for a survey."

While all this early work was going on at the Rambler and the Victor, in fact, during all the years George and I would eventually spend in the west, I made frequent flying visits back east to attend to the affairs of my company and the Prospectors and Developers Association. By the late 1940s, I had expanded the annual P.D.A. convention into a three-day affair, and established a pattern that is still followed to this day. The convention is always held early in March, beginning on a Monday, which enables out-of-town members to gather in Toronto at the weekend, and perhaps enjoy some socializing with friends they only meet once a year. We chose March as the best time because it usually marks the start of the spring "break-up," when few prospectors are likely to be in the bush. Also, it is early enough in the season for our members to be able to make plans to take advantage of any information they pick up at the convention. This could be either from the lecturers who give papers on new developments in mining, or the displays of maps and technical equipment that became part of the proceedings.

I always gave a great deal of care and attention to the selection

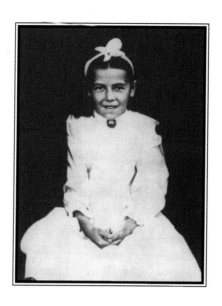

Viola MacMillan (christened Violet Rita Huggard)
– Windermere, c. 1909

Viola's parents: Harriet (Spiers) and Thomas Huggard
– Windermere, 1926

Phillip Proctor, George and Viola MacMillan –
Three Arch Bay, California, 1937

Viola staking claims in Hislop Township

Viola MacMillan – 1938

Viola always enjoyed an active lifestyle

Viola at bush camp

Viola – Timmins, 1940

Viola points to her claims – 1941-42

George, Tony Rice, Dr. J. Willis Ambrose, Viola,
Jolliffe, William Timm – 1942

Attending one of many social functions

Viola and George shared a love of prospecting

Hollinger Consolidated Gold Mines

Poster drafted for the war effort while George MacMillan was president of the P.D.A. from 1941 to 1943

Mining dynamo and belle of the ball

Viola – 1947

Viola breathed new life into the P.D.A. with her
energy and enthusiasm

Murdoch Mosher, George, Robert S. Palmer, Viola (seated),
Ambrose, Mrs. Palmer, not identified – 1947

Viola is front and centre among her peers at a 1950 P.D.A. convention

Viola speaks at a banquet – 1956

G.C. "Slim" Monture, Viola, Harrison – Lake Cinch opening,
September 1957

Viola and George attending the
Windfall Royal Commission hearings

Viola and Bill James – Canadian Mining Hall of Fame, 1991

Viola celebrates the acquisition of the Pinch
collection, on display in the Viola MacMillan Mineral Gallery in
Ottawa, with then Governor-General Ramon Hnatyshyn – 1992

Viola and Franc Joubin

John Hansuld (President), Viola, Premier Frank McKenna (NB),
Franc Joubin – 1993 P.D.A. convention

Viola and MP John Fraser at ceremony celebrating Viola's
Order of Canada

of speakers to address our members, and looking back now, I am very proud of the calibre of the various experts who responded to my invitations to give papers. Sometimes, of course, notorious bores who had nothing important to say or people with axes to grind would try to wangle invitations to speak. I became very good at explaining that we already had a full slate of speakers booked for that year, but would certainly get in touch with them again at some later date, which I never specified. I once tried to count how many speakers had addressed the association during the years I was its president, but gave up when the total passed the thousand mark.

As I write this, I have before me the program for our 15th annual convention in March 1947. As usual, the Monday morning was occupied by a business session, with elections of the executive committee and officers, and reports by the chairmen of committees set up to keep our members up to date. Information would be on such things as changes in provincial mining acts, regulations governing staking, and, on this occasion, an explanation of new regulations governing the sale of mining securities in Ontario.

By this time it was becoming more or less a matter of course that I would be re-elected president by acclamation, but I think it was still some time before the custom was adopted of greeting my election with a raucous chorus of "Let Me Call You Sweetheart." I still don't know who started that particular tradition, but he certainly caused me some embarrassment through the years!

The guest speaker for the welcoming luncheon in the banquet hall of the Royal York, at that 1947 convention, was Dr. R.M. Weidenhammer, of the U.S. Department of Commerce in Washington, D.C. Next, our members gathered in the concert hall for four lectures. The first of these was an account of prospecting possibilities in the Patricia district of northern Ontario by J.S. Satterly, a well-known Ontario Department of Mines geologist. This was followed by a review of the Manitoba mineral industry by a provincial geologist, a report on prospecting possibilities in the Northwest Territories by a federal government geologist, and an update on developments in the Noranda district by the Quebec government's resident geologist for that area.

I won't risk boring you by giving you the whole program in detail, but just to indicate its variety, the next morning was devoted to lectures on geophysics which, while it is extremely important to modern mineral exploration, was then only in its infancy. The program that evening included a round-table discussion of mine financing, an illustrated lecture on mining in Kenya Colony, and "Mining Day Programme," a CBC recording, because there was no television yet.

This was a reference to a pet project of mine for years which, I'm sorry to say, never really caught on outside the P.D.A. As I mentioned earlier, even before I was elected president of the association in 1944, I was convinced that Canadians were largely unaware of the importance of the mining industry to the country's welfare. Few of them realized, I'm sure, that in the last pre-war year, 1939, our mineral exports exceeded the total value of our farm exports by more than $100 million. In 1942, which was a peak year for mining production, the country's total mineral output was worth $566 million, well over the total of $334 million produced by the fisheries, fur, and forest industries combined.

But it's hard to get most people interested in statistics. Fortunately, I was not alone in my concern for the future of the mining industry. Toward the end of the war, for instance, the chief geologist of Canada, Dr. George Hanson, went on record as saying there was an urgent need for the Geological Survey to be expanded to at least five times its size at that time, if the country's immense resources were to be adequately mapped.

Other people were beginning to worry about how jobs could be found for all the servicemen who would soon be returning home, when there was no further need for the products of all the armament factories that had sprung up during the war. Fortunately, I came across a study done in the United States which concluded that one man employed in a mine kept 12 men in jobs elsewhere, producing food, clothing, timber, blasting powder, rails, drill steel, and all the 101 items needed to operate a mine.

Clearly, education was the key. This made it all the more strange that virtually nothing was being taught in Canadian schools about mining, minerals, or indeed the earth sciences generally. As a consequence, young people were making little or no attempt to enter the mining profession as mining engineers, geologists, or even prospectors. The Ontario government had even closed the one institution outside the universities that had done anything at all to prepare young people for a career in mining, the Haileybury School of Mines. A flood of protests from the mining industry soon forced it to reopen. The P.D.A. was among those who complained about this short-sighted policy, and we went even further, urging the government to open more mining colleges elsewhere in the province.

Having become so fascinated myself by what might be called the elements of mining — the study of the earth we live on, how it was formed, what it is made of, how the hills and streams and lakes and seas and mountains that surround us were formed — I could not understand the general lack of interest on the part of others. But how to combat this lack was a question.

Gradually, I came up with the idea of holding an annual Mining Day across the country, when there could be radio programs, special addresses, school projects and so forth, all focused on mining and its importance to the country. The association's executive committee supported my idea enthusiastically when I put it to them, and at our 1946 convention I was able to announce the formation of a Mining Day Fund, and invite all those interested to make a contribution to it. "The fund will be used," I told the convention's closing banquet that year, "to promote plans for the annual Mining Day and to get information on Canadian mining into the schools. We have received so much encouragement from educational authorities that we cannot help but feel that our plan is worthwhile."

Everything went swimmingly at first, and as I mentioned earlier, delegates at our 1947 convention were able to listen to a CBC radio Mining Day program. I also received and read out to the delegates several messages of support for the concept, including one from Prime Minister Mackenzie King.

But somehow, the idea never caught on in the country as a

whole, and after a while the celebration of Mining Day was left to us in the association. Instead of the nation-wide event I had hoped to make it, this became merely a label for the closing day of our annual convention.

I also continued my efforts to make women feel welcome at the association's convention, by introducing special lunches for them, addressed by women speakers from a variety of fields, and other events designed to keep them occupied and interested while their menfolk were attending the technical sessions. There were still, of course, those diehards among the men who felt that women had no place at the convention, or in the affairs of the association gener-ally. But I'm glad to say they found it much harder to sustain their position after the 1946 convention.

Part of the festivities that year was a "Prospector's I.Q. Quiz," in which the several hundred contestants were faced with 36 ore samples from different mines, and challenged to identify which mine each sample had come from and the approximate grade of its metal. To the absolute astonishment of everyone present, and my delight, Bertha Anson-Cartwright, the wife of a well-known con-sulting geologist and prospector, tied for first place in the contest with professional geologist G.M. Robson. I don't know whether her triumph caused any repercussions in the Anson-Cartwright household, but her husband Reg, who had presumably taught her most of what she knew about minerals, could only manage to take third place in the contest.

Of course, while everyone had lots of fun at the association's conventions through the years, most of the time was taken up by serious business. I found myself going further and further afield, as I made speeches hoping to advance the interests of the association and the mining industry in general.

For instance, as guest speaker for the closing banquet at our 1947 convention I managed to land Robert S. Palmer, executive director and secretary of the influential Colorado Mining Associa-tion. An indication of the importance attached to his visit to Canada was that the federal Minister of Mines and Resources, J.A. Glen, came to Toronto from Ottawa to introduce him. And before he left to return to the United States, Bob Palmer invited me to go to Denver the following February to speak at the 51st annual convention of his association.

I'll never forget the friendly reception those Americans gave me. They had bought a Canadian flag by mail order from some place in Toronto, and when they introduced me and I got up to speak, they put out all the lights in the hall except for a spotlight on the flag, which they had waving in a breeze whipped up by a fan carefully placed beside it. It was a wonderful moment. They presented the flag to me afterward, and I still have it carefully folded away in a box among my keepsakes.

I won't bother to repeat what I said on that occasion in any detail, because much of it now seems badly outdated; for instance, the big news in Canadian mining in those days was iron, with the tremendous Steep Rock development in Ontario, and the immense resources of Ungava and Labrador, which were just coming into prominence. Sadly, though, as we know, iron mining has all but ceased in this country, because of the way the world has changed since then.

But I think my essential message to the Colorado Mining Association all those years ago still holds true. I said that the problems facing mining had long since expanded beyond local and state horizons, indeed national horizons. They were now national and international in scope. For example, decisions made in the United States regarding almost any metal you could think of — gold, nickel, copper, or whatever — had profound effects on the Canadian mining industry. I said that the United States, as the world's greatest consumer of metals, and Canada, as the world's largest exporter of metals, could not avoid having the closest of interests.

Accordingly, I suggested the formation of an International Committee of Mining Organizations. "Such a committee," I said, "might consist of representatives from each member Association, that would meet at reasonable intervals to discuss problems of mutual interest, to explore questions of policy, and to promote national and international understanding of mining and its importance."

From the ovation I received when I sat down, I'm sure my

audience approved of this suggestion, but to the best of my knowledge the kind of committee I had suggested never came about. I still think my idea had validity, though. Just look at the way the various nations of the world, in recent years, have had to come together in trading groups just to be able to survive. Just after World War II, who would have thought that in only 40 years, all the different nations of Europe would form a Union. Who could have guessed that they would sink their national differences to form an economic force so powerful that it now seems to rival even the United States?

I am still not at all convinced that this free trade pact with the United States that Brian Mulroney got us into is going to be a good thing for Canada. I do know enough about the mining industry to know that Canada can't exist all by itself in a vacuum. We are affected by all sorts of developments, all over the world, and even though we can't necessarily control those developments, we surely must know about them, and take steps to accommodate ourselves to them. The alternative is nothing but trouble ahead for us. That is why I have always been such a strong believer in the exchange of ideas and information, and I continued to put forward my thoughts along these lines in speeches both at home and in the United States throughout my years as president of the P.D.A.

Some months after what I still consider was an important speech to the Colorado Mining Association in Denver, I attended another convention of mining men at San Francisco in the fall of 1948. On the way home to New Denver, I called in at Vancouver, where I was hoping to be able to negotiate an option on another property in the Slocan area, near the Victor and Rambler mines. I had had a very busy day and had gone to bed early when I was suddenly awakened by the telephone jangling beside my bed.

It was George. "Where on earth have you been?" he said, and I could tell he was excited. "I've been calling every hotel in the United States looking for you." I didn't bother to pick him up on this obvious exaggeration and contented myself by asking, "Okay, so now you've got me, what's all the fuss about?" Well, when he told me, I became as excited as he obviously was. "We've finally hit the main vein at the Victor," he said, "You'd better get back here as fast as you can."

Of course, I did just that, and George could hardly wait to take me into the mine to show me the vein. Mr. Doney, too, insisted on waiting until I got back before he would go in to see the find that eluded him all those years. George had tried to persuade him to go in and see it when they first found it, but dear old Mr. Doney had said, "No, I have got to go with Mrs. Mac. I'll wait till she gets back."

It was late in the day when I arrived home, and when we went into the mine, about ten o'clock at night, it was dark and we had miner's lamps on our hats. George led the way into the fourth level, with me following him and Mr. Doney coming along behind me. And when we came to the vein, I was so excited that I squealed and squealed like a stuck pig. It was just a solid wall of bluish-gray galena, the chief ore of lead. I had never seen anything like it before, and I threw my arms around Mr. Doney and said, "Oh Mr. Doney, I'm sorry it wasn't you who found it. You should have found it." But he replied, "Now Mrs. Mac. I told you I wanted you to make a million."

He was such a wonderful old man, and I was furious later when I found out that the company had retired him. But it was explained to me that he could never get used to all the machinery that came in as we expanded the Victor's operations, and there were worries he would fall under a bulldozer or something and get himself killed.

The new vein was found too late in the year to have much effect on our 1948 production. In that year, our total shipments of ore to the big Cominco smelter at Trail, about 60 miles to the south, amounted to only 220 tons, and part of that had been dug out by Mr. Doney before we took over the operation. But in 1949 we shipped almost eight times that amount — a total of 1,717 tons — more than the mine had produced in all the years it had been worked before it came into our hands. And that put $323,082 into the company's treasury.

In fact, by April 1949, the company was in the clear. We had paid Mrs. Robinson the remaining $25,000 she was owed, and recovered all our start-up costs. By that time, the work force had grown to 21 men, and we kept on expanding.

As the ore was removed from the fourth level, George and I began to go down the mountain, picking suitable spots to open up new levels. And that marvellous vein just kept on going deeper and deeper. Each time we opened a new level and found the vein again the miners from miles around would gather for a party to celebrate.

As our operations expanded, the old log buildings had to go, of course. We had to have a proper cookery up there for the men. We ultimately had about 80 men working at the Victor, and we built a totally new camp. We had to bulldoze out part of the side of the mountain to get enough level space to build on, and I remember when we were about to open the new buildings. It was Christmas-time and the men were away on holiday. I was looking around the dining room, and I decided the view down the valley was so terrific that all the benches should face the windows.

Also, in any mining camp I had ever been in, the tables had always seemed to be black or some other dull color. That wasn't good enough for me. I told George, "No, I like tulip red. It's exciting, and it makes you feel like eating. Tulip red is very attractive." So I got a bunch of paint and set to work and by the time the men came back the dining room just looked wonderful. And in one corner I had a big sort of tropical plant that went almost up to the ceiling.

As our production continued to increase, our receipts continued to grow year by year. In 1953, the Victor's peak production year, our "gross smelter returns" as they called them in the books, amounted to $1,427,134.64. That year, just to show you how that mine grew after we took it over from poor Mr. Doney, we shipped more than 27,000 tons of ore, which yielded the following quantities of metals: almost eight million pounds of lead, more than four million pounds of zinc, more than half a million ounces of silver, 25,000 pounds of cadmium, and even 217 ounces of gold.

CHAPTER
FOURTEEN

I have never been happier, or busier, than I was during the 1950s. Those were glory years for me, and even though they ended up taking a serious toll on my health, I don't regret them one bit.

As the profits began to come in from the Victor's ore, I decided, and everyone associated with the company agreed with me, that they should be ploughed back into the company's development and not paid out in dividends at that early stage. That view was apparently shared by outside investors in ViolaMac, judging from the way the prices paid for its shares on the Toronto Stock Exchange rose steadily after it was initially listed in 1949.

The first thing we were able to do as the smelter receipts flowed in was to build our own mill at the mine. Until that opened in December 1950, we had been shipping only our top-quality ore, known as "clean lead," to the smelter at Trail. But the mine also produced a lot of lower-grade ore that was not economical to ship to the smelter in its raw state. However, with the mill operating, we were able to process the lower-grade ore into lead and zinc concentrates, which we were soon shipping in 40-ton car loads to the smelter for refining. This added substantially to our smelter receipts.

I spoke earlier in this book about the way mining companies enter joint ventures to share the risks of new developments. This is also, of course, an accepted way for a mining company to grow, either by buying into a company which appears to have a likely-looking prospect, or even buying it out completely. And as ViolaMac's smelter receipts continued to increase, I was constantly on the lookout for new opportunities.

Over the next few years, ViolaMac acquired control of, or bought a substantial interest in, well over a dozen other companies. For technical reasons too complicated to go into here, the share holdings in those companies would usually be divided between ViolaMac itself, and a wholly-owned subsidiary I set up as a financial and investment holding company, and called after my birthplace, Deebank Ltd. And sometimes I would buy some shares on my own account.

Anyone who lived in the west in the '50s will remember the excitement of those early days of the Alberta oil boom, which followed Imperial Oil's famous discovery well at Leduc in 1947. George and I needed no convincing about the importance of diversification to a company. After all, ViolaMac had been set up in the hope of mining gold, but here we were, doing very nicely thank you, by mining lead and silver.

So, on ViolaMac's behalf I formed a company called Camarillo Oils Limited, and negotiated some joint ventures with other companies holding oil leases in various parts of Alberta. I remember how thrilled George and I were once when we were in Calgary and a member of the drilling crew came to our hotel and got us out of bed late one night. He told us they had made a strike at a place called Oliver Lake, so we drove there with him right away. Unfortunately, as so many hopefuls looking to become oil millionaires found in those days, we had struck natural gas, not oil. And since there was no market for gas in those days, we just had to cap that well, and I'm afraid we never found another one.

But oil was a little out of our real field of mining, and the big excitement in mining in the early '50s was uranium. So naturally we tried very hard to put ViolaMac into the uranium business. Even though we made a number of false starts, which is only par for the course in the mining game, we were eventually successful.

But in the spring of 1953, the pace of the life I had been leading, back and forth between the west and Toronto, had begun to catch up on me. I was nearing 50 years old, of course, and after a routine medical check-up my doctor told me I had a heart murmur, warned me to slow down, and advised me to get away on a long holiday. So George and I booked a stateroom on the Queen Mary out of New York for a vacation in Europe. The itinerary included grandstand seats from which we were to watch the procession for the Coronation of our present Queen.

By now we had an excellent manager looking after things at the Victor mine, Jack Black, but at the last minute some problem came up that meant George had to cancel his holiday. I didn't want to go without him but he insisted I carry through with our plans, and so I found myself steaming out of New York all alone in this huge stateroom with two beds. And so many people sent me flowers that the place reminded me of a funeral parlour.

Everyone was very nice to me on the way over, though, and I was beginning to relax by the time we got to Le Havre, but then we weren't allowed to get off the ship right away because of some strike by longshoremen. They got that sorted out eventually, and a representative of the tourist agency we had booked with saw me on the train to Paris where I had a marvellous room at the famous George the Fifth Hotel.

And there, two very good old friends turned up to salvage my vacation. Bob Farquharson was a famous Toronto editor I had known since before the war, who was at that time director of information at N.A.T.O. headquarters in Paris. He and his wife Ricka had attended many parties at my Oriole Parkway home. And from then on I had a wonderful time. Ricka dropped everything to show me Paris, then went with me on a tour of the Swiss Alps, and over to the U.K. where we got as far as Scotland and saw the famous St. Andrew's golf course. I played a little golf myself down in Florida in those days, but I didn't dare set foot on those hallowed St. Andrew's links!

Our original tour also called for a visit to Italy, but by this time I was getting lonely. It wasn't the same without George to enjoy it, so I headed back home. But George wouldn't hear of us missing the Coronation, after we had managed to get seats right outside Buckingham Palace. So he insisted on me setting sail again for London, this time from Montreal, and said he would fly over in time to join me for the great day. This time C.D. Howe and a lot of other people I knew from Ottawa were among the passengers, and I was beginning to feel like a veteran ocean traveller. I arrived in London in time to attend a huge garden party at the palace.

George joined me at the hotel the day before we were due to take our seats in the stands at the unearthly hour of five in the morning, or thereabouts. I wasn't dressed for the London weather, which was damp and chilly so early in the day, and as the time for the parade approached, I was violently ill. Fortunately, we had spotted two of the doctors from Women's College Hospital sitting a couple of rows ahead of us. I knew them from my work on the hospital board, and George went down and told them I was in a bad way. Those two girls came up and thank goodness they had outfitted themselves with a first-aid kit in the shape of a flask of brandy. After a healing dose of that, I felt better and was able to enjoy that once-in-a-lifetime spectacle, which I still remember with great pleasure.

When I got back home, I was no more able to stop working than I was able to stop breathing. We had bought some uranium claims in Saskatchewan before my trip to Europe, and we went on looking for more after my return.

The story of uranium in Canada, which was an important one for our post-war prosperity, doesn't begin with uranium at all, but with radium, another radioactive substance. It goes back long before the war and the terrible shock of the atomic bombs on Hiroshima and Nagasaki.

The chief actor in the story was a man who later became a good friend of mine, Gilbert LaBine, a great supporter of the P.D.A. and our president in 1936. Gilbert, with his older brother and lifelong partner Charlie, were born on a farm near Pembroke in the Ottawa Valley. They worked in the silver mines at Cobalt in the early days and did some prospecting on the side. With some money he made from a silver discovery, Gilbert put himself through the Haileybury School of Mines, and after Charlie got back from the First World War, they went out west. They formed Eldorado Gold Mines Ltd. to work some claims they staked in Manitoba. Even though the ore soon ran out, their company made enough money to finance them in some more prospecting.

In 1930, Gilbert had himself flown into the shore of Great Bear Lake, which straddles the Arctic Circle in the Northwest Territories, 1,000 miles north of Edmonton. There he found a rich deposit of pitchblende. If he had not taken that early training at the Haileybury school, he would probably never have recognized the dark brown, almost black substance he came across as pitchblende and realized that it might contain radium.

At that time, treatment with radium was the last hope for some sufferers from cancer, and it was so scarce that the world price for it was something like two million dollars an ounce. When government assays confirmed that Gilbert's pitchblende was very rich, and that it did indeed contain radium, he and Charlie were able to raise financing to develop a mine in that wilderness. Everything they needed had to be either flown in or shipped in during the short summer season.

By 1933 they had built a mill that had to process 50 tons of ore to finish up with one ton of concentrate, that took the form of a black powder. Seven tons of various chemicals were needed to refine one ton of this powder, so Eldorado built its refinery within reach of a supply of the chemicals at Port Hope, on the shore of Lake Ontario east of Toronto. To get from the mine to Port Hope, the concentrates had to be shipped 1,500 miles by barge across Great Bear Lake, up the Mackenzie River, across the corner of Great Slave Lake, and from there up the Slave and Athabasca rivers to the nearest railroad terminal at a place called Waterways, near Fort McMurray in northern Alberta. Then it was still a 3,000-mile rail journey to Port Hope.

It was one of the most remarkable mining achievements in history. But the odds were against it from the start. It was late in 1936 before the company's total production added up to a single ounce of radium. In the process, it produced hundreds of tons of uranium, which was considered to be waste, since there was certainly no market for it. Uranium just accumulated in an apparently worthless stockpile at the refinery.

The outbreak of the war added to Eldorado's problems, and the LaBine brothers closed their mine in 1940. But as the war progressed, they began to get surprise orders for uranium, and in 1941, at C.D. Howe's request, Gilbert reopened the mine. And this time, in great secrecy, its concentrates were flown south to Port Hope and refined into uranium for use in the atomic-bomb project, though no one knew that at the time. Later still, in the interests of national security, the government decided to expropriate Eldorado and it became a government company, though Gilbert was left in place to operate it.

Even before the war ended, with the poor Japanese acting as guinea pigs for the tragic demonstration of the destructive power locked up in the atoms of uranium, our allies were anxious to make sure they would have adequate supplies of that metal to ensure their defense in the post-war years. So the government put teams of prospectors into the field to look for it under Gilbert's direction. And Ottawa retained tight control over all aspects of the uranium industry — prospecting, development, and production — as the Cold War took the place of the peace we had all been hoping for.

But in 1948, when the officially-sponsored search seemed to be having very little effect, the federal authorities opened the way for private enterprise to go into prospecting for uranium and developing mines if any potentially profitable sources of it were found. I remember that for some time before then, I had made several speeches on behalf of the P.D.A. urging the government to open the field to private interests.

When the government first announced that private prospectors could explore for uranium deposits, there was a rush of staking, and some promising discoveries. But the government still insisted on buying all uranium produced by private industry, and at first the price was set too low to persuade development money to take the risks involved in setting up new mines.

Then in 1950, with a promise by Washington to buy all the uranium Canada could produce, Ottawa set a new price of ten dollars a pound for uranium above a certain grade. This was way above the old price it had been prepared to pay, and private entrepreneurs began to show more interest. Among them were the LaBine brothers, who had resigned from Eldorado to go prospecting again when the government threw the business open to private enterprise. A prospector working for them, Ed Zeemel, soon found another rich uranium deposit near the shore of Lake Athabasca, in the northwest corner of Saskatchewan, not far from another discovery the Eldorado company had made in the Beaverlodge area.

Gilbert and Charlie put their new claims into another of their gold properties, Gunnar Mines, and the news of their success sparked a huge staking rush into the Beaverlodge area in the early '50s. I remember there was a lot of interest in Canadian mining in Europe while I was on my vacation in 1953, and I told everyone who asked me for a good tip, "Buy Gunnar." And if they did, they wouldn't have been sorry, because Gilbert and Charlie built Gunnar into what was for a while the largest single uranium producer in North America.

So when I heard that a company called Glencair Mining Co. Ltd. had a group of claims tying onto the Gunnar property to the south I immediately became interested in it. Glencair was owned by Stephen Roman, who had not yet become famous in Canadian mining circles. When I heard he wanted to sell, I immediately began to negotiate with him on behalf of ViolaMac. We thought at the time that the Gunnar ore body was dipping down to the south, and Gilbert and Charlie must have thought so too, because they came in with me on the deal. In all, ViolaMac paid Roman something like half a million dollars for Glencair, with Gilbert and Charlie each putting up $25,000 of that amount as their share. I have always believed it was that money that enabled Steve Roman to buy control of Denison Mines, which of course he built into a huge mining empire, but only after he finally managed to develop his own uranium mine in the Algoma area of Ontario.

Much to our disappointment, though, Gunnar's ore did not

carry on over to the Glencair ground, and while we held on to the property, we were never able to develop it into a mine. Our next venture into the uranium field was brought to us by a prospector named Walter Blair, who had scored some success with a company called Chimo Gold Mines in Quebec. Walter had been drawn into the Beaverlodge excitement and had staked some claims neighbouring the Gunnar, and which Gilbert and Charlie wanted. He received a sizeable block of Gunnar shares in return for them.

Walter had also staked ten claims along the north shore of Lake Athabasca, about 25 miles northwest of the Gunnar property, and had obtained some radioactive showings on them. When we first started discussing a deal, I had Dr. Ambrose examine his ground, and as a result of his report we formed a company called Uranium Ridge Mines Ltd. The name came to me at the time we were considering the deal, while George and I were camped on a ridge in the Beaverlodge area looking for prospects. The way the company was set up, ViolaMac and Chimo took 25% each in the initial stages, with the rest of the shares available for the public. Later though, ViolaMac bought more shares and gained control.

Right at the start, and on the basis of Dr. Ambrose's report, Uranium Ridge took an option on 20 more claims adjoining Walter's claims to the west, which were owned by a company called Urex Mines, so that the property eventually stretched for two miles along the north shore of the lake. Uranium Ridge Mines was formed in the fall of 1953, and we immediately set up a winter camp in preparation for a program of drilling through the lake ice once the freeze-up permitted.

That drilling was well under way when I was able to report a record year to ViolaMac's shareholders at the annual general meeting early in 1954. The company's net earnings for the year were $358,937, a satisfying increase of more than $66,000 on the previous year. The company's working capital, even after its expenditures on the other activities I have mentioned above, stood at almost half a million dollars.

There was just one thing that had been giving me growing concern for some time now. With all the expansion that had been going on, it was obvious that the company had long outgrown my old MacMillan Securities office at 67 Yonge. I was still running the P.D.A. from my own office, and with its membership now approaching 2,000, Miss Graham, Mrs. Drewe, and the rest of my staff hardly had room to turn around. So when the chance came to lease space in a brand-new brick and aluminum building at 25 Adelaide Street West, I jumped at it. That building has been torn down now to make way for one of the many skyscrapers in that area, but in its day it was considered the last word in office buildings, partly because of what was still a novelty at that time: it had an apartment on the top floor, the 13th.

One day I needed to see the two partners who owned the building about something, and I was told they were on the top floor. So I took the elevator up there and found them in some sort of argument. My arrival quieted them down, and I gathered they could not agree about what to do with the apartment. I think the son of one of the partners wanted it, and expected to pay a very low rent or none at all, and neither of the partners thought that was a very good idea. So they suggested I should rent it. I laughed them off at first. "Why," I said, "my home is only ten minutes away from here by cab." But they told me what a novelty my "penthouse" would be, how useful it would be for entertaining clients, how convenient if I had to work late as I usually did when there was a snowstorm on.

Well, they must have been good salesmen, because I eventually agreed to take the place. I had a lot of fun decorating and furnishing it, and I think George did, too. It was not very big, but we made it look much bigger by lining some of the walls with mirrors, and we knocked out a wall between two small rooms to create a spacious L-shaped living room. At my insistence, the dominant colour scheme was pink, but we accented that in places by painting some of the walls a very nice shade of dove grey, and covering others with a dark green textured wallpaper.

The novelty of a couple who could commute to work by elevator — ViolaMac's office was down on the fourth floor — soon attracted attention in the press. I was often interviewed in those days, as the lady president of a company that had already produced ore worth more than $3.5 million and would go on to produce much more in future years. And now, having two homes in Toronto, we finally sold the farm out north of Oakville, which we had been thinking of doing for some time, because that area was becoming built up and it was getting more and more difficult to hire reliable farm help.

Pleasant though my now penthouse was, and it certainly did prove a great convenience in some of my business dealings, George and I did not spend very much time there in those early days. There was still too much to do out west.

The 10,000 feet of drilling, carried out for us on the Uranium Ridge property during the winter of 1954, produced only disappointing results, so we dropped the option on the Urex claims adjoining our original ground. But that summer we picked up 12 more claims known as the Tamlyn-Pitche group, in the heart of the Beaverlodge area at the southwest end of Beaverlodge Lake.

Surface exploration and some drilling done by the previous owners of the claims had indicated nine separate radioactive zones. By the fall, we had set up a permanent camp and put a crew to work to develop one of those zones which, according to an engineer's report we obtained, was expected to contain more than 5,000 tons of ore.

Uranium fever was still at its height in 1954, so when an opportunity arose that fall to purchase another promising prospect, I lost no time in trying to acquire it for ViolaMac. Cinch Lake Uranium Mines Ltd. had been incorporated in 1949 to hold eight claims staked in the Beaverlodge area a year earlier, by a prospector named Charles Swenson.

A drilling program had outlined two radioactive zones bearing considerable tonnage, but the company's owner, Arthur Davidson, an executive of a Windsor machine-tool company, was apparently not impressed by the grade of the ore because he had decided to sell out. He readily accepted my offer, which was an immediate purchase of 200,000 shares at 30 cents, or a total of $60,000, with

options which, if they were all taken up, would eventually give
ViolaMac control of the company.

I closed the deal in October 1954, reorganized the company,
changed its name to Lake Cinch Mines, and set about planning a
new drilling program that I hoped would lead to a contract to
supply uranium to the Crown-owned Eldorado.

CHAPTER
FIFTEEN

One morning around the time that I was negotiating the Lake Cinch deal, I was going downtown on the bus from my Oriole Parkway home when I ran into one of Noranda's exploration men I knew. I told him about my plans and he said, "Oh, you're going to be disappointed there. We did a lot of work on that property and didn't find anything worthwhile." So I said, "Yes, but you didn't work down into the lake." He replied, "Oh no. The fault's not down there." Well, everyone's entitled to his own opinion, so I just said, "You may not think so, but that's where I'm going to drill."

You see, I had walked all over that property before we bought it, and there was something about the geology down toward the lake that just gave me a hunch we would find a fault down there. So that was where I gave instructions to spot the first hole we drilled in our new program. As soon as the ice was thick enough the program got under way, and our very first hole struck good ore, richer than anything that had been found on the property previously.

So of course we kept on drilling, and the more we drilled the more encouraging the results became. By late May of 1955, Viola-Mac was firmly in control of Lake Cinch. The original schedule of options called for us to purchase shares in installments, at prices ranging from a bottom of 30 cents each up to a final price of $1.25. The last option was to have been exercisable on October 5, 1956. Instead, we were so optimistic that we had exercised all our options by that May, which gave us 1.8 million Lake Cinch shares, and put $800,000 into the company's treasury.

By that fall, we were so confident we had a mine in the making that we had sunk a 500-foot shaft and were driving cross-cuts into the rock at the 300- and 500-foot levels. The underground results, when the ore was analyzed, proved to be even better than our surface exploration had indicated they would be.

The federal authorities had set a deadline of March 1956 for the signing of new supply contracts with Eldorado, and we pushed the work ahead as fast as possible so as to be sure we would be well equipped with facts and figures to justify our expectations for the mine, when the time came to negotiate with Eldorado.

In the meantime, our excellent staff under Jack Black at the Victor kept on finding new ore shoots, and in mid-1955 it seemed that the exploration we had been carrying out on our neighbouring Lane Bachelor property was about to bear fruit. The geologists had uncovered three veins on the fourth level of the old mine which at first appeared similar to those that had served us so well in the main mine, and for a time we thought we might be able to start making some shipments to the smelter from the Lone Bachelor. Sadly, as time would tell, that was not to be.

But the grand old Victor continued to produce handsomely for us. Our gross smelter receipts for 1955 were only a shade under the record total we had achieved in 1953, and in 1956, while somewhat lower, they were still well over a million dollars. So we were able to go on acquiring new properties in our attempt to diversify the company's interests.

For a long time we held high hopes for a group of claims we picked up in the base metal area near Bathurst, New Brunswick, which was enjoying quite a boom at that time. We also found some traces of copper on some claims we bought at Cirrus Creek, about 20 miles southwest of another booming base metals area, Manitouwadge, in northwestern Ontario.

Also, in 1955, there was a sudden upsurge in interest in a soft, silver-white metal called lithium, which among other things is the lightest metal known to man. The first orbiting spacecraft, the Russians' Sputnik, was still a couple of years in the future, and it would be a full 14 years before Americans walked on the moon. But already there was a feeling that there were great things ahead for the infant science of rocketry, which the Germans had pioneered with their v-1 and v-2 weapons during World War II. And people thought lithium would somehow find an important place in that developing science.

It didn't happen quite that way, and as far as I know the main uses for lithium nowadays are in lubricating greases and in strengthening aluminum for the aircraft manufacturing industry. But it's an old bromide that hindsight is the clearest form of 20/20 vision, and back in 1955, lithium was generally thought to have a great future. So the mining press reacted with great enthusiasm when I was able to acquire for ViolaMac a 20-claim group covering 1,000 acres at Cat Lake, about 35 miles northeast of Lac du Bonnet, in the heart of a new lithium belt that was making headlines in Manitoba. Preliminary work on the property had indicated nine lithium showings. When we acquired the claims in May of 1955, George went up there to take charge of the work and supervise the construction of a camp to house a crew of 18 men, including two geologists. And we promptly commissioned a drilling program for that summer.

The drilling results were so favourable that we enlarged the property by staking 11 neighbouring claims, and continued our exploration. By the fall, the drills had outlined an estimated four million tons of ore grading an average of 1.3% lithia. Analysis showed the ore to be low in manganese and iron content, which made it particularly desirable. So early in 1956, I cast around for outside partners and formed a separate company to acquire the property, Lithia Mines & Chemicals Ltd., with ViolaMac retaining control. The property was located six miles from an all-weather road and eight miles from an existing electric power line. The new company immediately entered negotiations with the Manitoba government to extend both these facilities into where we planned to sink a shaft to develop the mine.

As I told the annual general meeting of shareholders in April 1956, ViolaMac was now more than ever a growth company. I was pleased to be able to report a record net profit for 1955 of $442,316. This worked out to 15 cents per share, an increase of 46% over the previous year.

I also reported to the shareholders that our subsidiary company, Lake Cinch, had made a formal application to Eldorado for a contract to supply it with uranium concentrates. At that time, for security reasons, I was not able to disclose the extent of the ore reserves our exploration had outlined, the grade of the ore, the tonnage involved, or the rate at which we expected to be able to make shipments. But privately we were pretty sure we had enough ore of very high grade. The estimate was that it would average at least six pounds of uranium oxide to the ton. We were reasonably confident of securing the contract. At that time, in fact, we thought our operation might be so big that it would justify us building our own mill to process the ore. But when the contract was negotiated and signed that summer, it called for us to ship our ore to a custom mill being built near our mine by a company called Lorado Uranium Mines. The contract directed us to supply ore containing a million and a half pounds of uranium oxide, for which we would be paid $15.75 million, with the shipments to be completed by the end of February 1962.

With all the preparatory work we had done, we were ready to begin shipping ore before the mill was completed and able to accept it. When our shipments finally began, in May 1957, we started off at the rate of 75 tons a day, to enable the mill management to tune up its operation. But late in the year, when the mill was ready, we were able to double our shipments to 150 tons a day.

All told that first year, we shipped a little over 17,000 tons of ore, which brought the company $532,427. In our first full year of operation, 1958, we shipped 52,000 tons of ore, which brought in $1.7 million after milling charges, and Lake Cinch registered a profit for the year of $527,803.

This was particularly welcome news, for by that time it was beginning to look as though the Victor mine was at last reaching the end of the road. We had noticed a drop in production during 1957, when our ore shipments were about 4,000 tons below the previous year's level, and our gross smelter receipts dropped below the million-dollar mark for the first time since 1953.

The production drop was even more drastic during 1958. Our lead shipments fell from 4.4 million pounds all the way down to 2.2 million pounds, and our zinc production slumped even more, from 5.1 million pounds down to 1.4 million pounds. That year our total shipments only amounted to just over 9,000 tons, the lowest figure since 1952, and our gross smelter receipts were only $418,917, less than half what they had been a year earlier.

Therefore, our efforts to diversify ViolaMac took on even more urgency, and so far Lake Cinch had been our only success in that direction. The Bathurst base-metal claims had not worked out, and so far no buyers had been found for our lithium, which remained in the ground as the bloom seemed to be fading from the lithium rose. Work was more or less at a standstill also on Uranium Ridge, for which we had not been able to secure a sales contract.

Then Lady Luck smiled on me once again, in the shape of a totally unexpected phone call from an old friend in the Porcupine, where I had started out what now seemed so many years ago. George Jamieson was a veteran prospector who had staked some ground about 14 miles west of Timmins for a local syndicate back in the early 1920s. They had managed to sell their claims to Hollinger Gold Mines, which developed a mine called the Kam-Kotia on them, but then for some reason did not operate it. By arrangement with Hollinger, the government's War Time Metals organization mined about 200,000 tons of copper ore from the Kam-Kotia during the war. But then Hollinger let the mine sit idle again; I guess it was too small to really spark their interest.

Years before George Jamieson called me, I had tried to persuade Jules Timmins, the head of Hollinger, to sell me the Kam-Kotia. Jules said he would if I could get an option on some neighbouring claims that George Jamieson still owned. No doubt he was just trying to put me off, because all sorts of people had tried to buy those claims from George and he had always refused to sell them.

But here he was, one morning early in 1959, calling me in my Toronto office and asking, "You're going to be in Timmins tomorrow aren't you, you and George?" In actual fact, George and I had planned to visit friends in Chicago that weekend, but something in Jamieson's tone of voice made me reply, "Yes, George, we are." He sounded pleased, and said, "Good, I'll be looking for you to come out and see me."

As soon as he got off the phone, I dashed into the geological room, where George and Dr. Ambrose were having some kind of a technical discussion and I told George, "We've got to be in Timmins tomorrow. George Jamieson just called me and I think he wants to make a deal on his property."

Well, George knew how important that could be, so he didn't quibble about missing our trip to Chicago. But when we woke up in our Timmins hotel room next morning, there was about two feet of snow on the ground and George didn't fancy the idea of driving out to Jamieson's place in our rented car. So Jamieson got someone to drive him into town and came to our room.

And sure enough, he was finally willing to part with his claims abutting on the Kam-Kotia property, and asked me to draw up an agreement for him to sign. ''Well, what kind of a deal can we make?'' I asked him. "Oh, you know what to do," he replied. "Just fix it up." So we bargained a bit and agreed on a price.

I hadn't yet worked out which company it would be best to put the option into, so I drew up a simple agreement transferring the claims from George Jamieson to George MacMillan, and Jamieson came to our room again next day to sign it; George was still in bed, I remember it being a Sunday morning, and I had to round up two of the hotel maids to witness the agreement.

As soon as Jamieson left I got on the phone to Jules Timmins in Montreal. I had forgotten he was a good Catholic, and it being Sunday morning, he was out at church. I had to call him back later.

When I finally reached him, I guess it was around lunchtime, I said, "Mr. Timmins, you remember you promised me that if I ever got George Jamieson's other property you'd make a deal with me on Kam-Kotia? Well, I signed with Jamieson this morning." Jules paused a moment and then said, "Yes, I did promise you that, didn't I? So we'll make a deal." He told me Percy Finlay, his lawyer, would be in Montreal next day, and he would tell him to get everything arranged and I could see Finlay in Toronto later that week.

I knew Percy well, he died just recently, and once Mr. Timmins had agreed to do the deal, the details didn't take long to arrange. In March 1959, ViolaMac purchased Hollinger's control block of Kam-Kotia Porcupine Mines: 33,000 shares, amounting to 82.5% of the company's issued capital, for a total of $198,000. And I made arrangements immediately for a drilling program to find out exactly what I had bought.

I knew from company records that previous work on the property had outlined 825,000 tons of ore grading 1.95% copper, 0.2% zinc, and 600,000 tons grading 0.5% copper and 4% zinc. The first holes drilled for ViolaMac indicated even better values than those, so much so that I commissioned a geophysical survey of the property right away.

Then once again George and I headed out west, where the news from the Victor was still not good. In fact, when all the results were in for that year, 1959, our gross smelter receipts were only $249,026, considerably less than they had been during our first full year of operations, ten years earlier.

By this time, as part of our diversification program, we had taken over and reorganized another old Slocan company, Carnegie Mines, and spent about $20,000 to reactivate its mill. This was now treating ore from the Victor and some other companies on a custom basis, and we were conducting geological explorations underground in the hope of being able to reopen the mine. But in accordance with accepted mining practice we were still searching for new acquisitions to replace the ageing Victor.

That summer, I had to go to Vancouver to discuss a possible

deal for a property with a well-known mining man, Mel O'Brien, and George decided to come with me. We had a couple of my brother Ed's children, and Katherine Ambrose, Dr. Ambrose's daughter, spending a holiday with us in New Denver. Kathy's mother had died and she was out west visiting an aunt. So we decided to take them with us on the drive to Vancouver.

I had not been feeling well before we left New Denver, and I felt much worse in Vancouver. We had no sooner arrived there than I told George, "I'm really not well. Let's go home." This was so unlike me that George got really worried and agreed right away.

He decided that the quickest way home was to dip down into the U.S., where the roads were better in those days, and cut back up into Canada south of Nelson, from where it was only a short distance home to New Denver. I'll never forget that drive. I was very, very ill, all the way. The kids were young, of course, and they wanted the radio on in the car. I just couldn't stand it, and I kept saying, "Oh, I wish you'd shut that radio off."

I got so bad that George wanted to stop and take me to a doctor when we were passing through a town in the States. I think it was Colville, in the northern part of Washington state. But I groaned, "No, let's get home." I was vomiting by that time, and when we got to Nelson, George put his foot down and insisted I see a doctor. The doctor took one look at me and rushed me into the hospital there, where they kept me for about a month.

Iris Black, the wife of our manager at the Victor, was a nurse and a friend of ours. We had been away on winter holidays to Florida together a couple of times. She came down to look after me, for which I was very grateful.

Eventually, the doctors decided I could fly home to Toronto, but I had to travel on a stretcher, and a doctor came with me. And it was not for quite a while after I had been recuperating at home, I think it was at least two months, before my own doctor let me get up and about and even contemplate showing my face in the office again. Then I was given the bad news.

My doctor told me I had had a heart attack, and that unless I wanted to sign my own death warrant, I must give up all my business activities forthwith and forever. I had had a lucky escape. I was nearing 60 years of age. The work I had always loved, helped along by Lady Luck, had made me financially independent. I should have paid better attention to that doctor.

CHAPTER
SIXTEEN

I agonized for weeks, trying to come to terms with the idea that I was going to have to sell ViolaMac. But early in 1960 when I accepted the inevitable, it was not the best of times to go looking for a buyer. By then it was more than ever clear that the Victor's days as a producing mine were numbered. And at the same time, the bottom had dropped out of the uranium market.

Our Lake Cinch mine shipped more ore during 1959 than the previous year, almost 56,000 tons, containing 267,866 pounds of uranium oxide. But because the ore was slightly lower in grade, it fetched a lower price, and our returns for the year were down to $1.3 million. Because of higher wages and freight rates, the profit for the year was down to $155,554.

But the fates had even worse in store for the Lake Cinch company. Late in 1959, the United States notified Canada that it would henceforth be able to satisfy all its uranium requirements from its own domestic sources, and consequently would not be renewing its Canadian contracts when they ran out in 1962. This was a terrible blow to the whole Canadian uranium industry. The federal government tried to cushion the impact on the mining companies, and the communities like Elliot Lake that depended on them, by introducing a "stretch-out" program to spread uranium deliveries over a longer period. But in the process, many contracts were cancelled and mines closed.

The Lorado company, which had been processing our Lake Cinch ore, was one of those that went under. Its quota and contracts were taken over by the government's Eldorado company. In return for cancellation of its contract, Lake Cinch received $2.5 million in two equal cash payments, but we had to close down the mine in March 1960, and sell its equipment for whatever we could get for it.

I'll never forget the day the first installment of that payment came in. It was a cheque for $1.25 million and it was a Saturday morning. As I couldn't put the cheque straight away into the bank, I tucked it into my purse with the other papers I always used to keep in there.

I had arranged to meet a friend at the King Edward Hotel, and we went into the coffee shop there for a chat. I put my purse down on the floor, right by my foot, as we had a coffee. And then we went off to another engagement over at the Royal York. We were halfway there when I suddenly gasped, "My God. I've left my purse in the coffee shop!"

I didn't dare to run back, because I was still having to take it easy after my heart attack, but you can bet I sure hurried! And you can imagine how relieved I was when I found my purse still resting beside the table just where I had left it. No one had touched it or the cheque inside it, but I made good and sure to get into the bank first thing on Monday morning.

So even though the outlook didn't look good for the Victor mine, when the time came to sell ViolaMac, the Lake Cinch treasury was bulging with cash. And the prospects for the Kam-Kotia looked very good indeed. The drilling program and the follow-up geophysical work we commissioned after I acquired the property from Jules Timmins had discovered an entirely new ore body that appeared to be 1,400 feet long and 150 wide, about 200 feet from the old deposit that had been worked during the war.

With the help of the experts, we had decided there was enough ore on the property to support an open-pit mining operation, producing 750 tons of ore a day. This was more than enough to generate a nice profit, and I set about looking for a mill to process it into copper and zinc concentrates. Building a new mill would have been too costly, so I cast about for a second-hand one we could buy at a reasonable price. I found what I was looking for at an old mine called the Nickel Rim in Sudbury, which had a mill standing idle that appeared to be in perfectly good shape.

I hired an engineer named George Miller to dismantle that mill, ship it to our Kam-Kotia property and rebuild it there. George was a wonderful old fellow, but it was strange to watch him on the phone. He was deaf, and he used to hold the phone to his chest, which was where he kept his hearing aid. To see George at work was marvellous. He knew where every nut and bolt went in that mill, numbered everything and after the whole works had been shipped to the Kam-Kotia, put it all back together again without a hitch.

Another property we were hoping might replace the Victor at around that time was Abino Gold Mines Ltd. Abino had been formed in 1939 by Albert Kay, who was the postmaster at McKenzie Island, in the Red Lake area of northwest Ontario. It had some promising-looking claims neighbouring what later became the fabulously rich Campbell Red Lake Gold Mine, and was surrounded by several other producing gold properties, including the Dickenson mine.

Kay and his group had done some drilling on the Abino property just after the war, but then had run out of money. Poor Albert was later killed in a freak accident, when he was crushed between a wharf and a boat that was docking at McKenzie Island. In just about the last deal I did for ViolaMac before I took sick, I put some financing into Abino through Deebank Ltd. and acquired management control of the company. We immediately commenced a drilling program and were so encouraged by the results that by the early part of 1960 we had sunk a shaft and begun to drive exploratory cross-cuts from it at the 200-, 350-, and 500-foot levels.

The shaft sinking was recommended to us by Chester Keryliw, a consulting geologist who specialized in the Red Lake area, and as a result of his exploration of the Abino property on our behalf, he came to the conclusion that it was underlain by a geological fold similar to the one that contained the gold at the nearby Dickenson mine. The Dickenson was one of the earliest, and certainly one of the most profitable ventures of the well-respected Toronto mining promoter Arthur W. White. And when news got around about the geological structure of the Abino property, Art White naturally became interested and contacted me.

When we began to talk, and I gave him some of the facts and figures about ViolaMac, he also became greatly interested in the prospects for the Kam-Kotia. I've no doubt that even though the Lake Cinch mine had been closed down by then, Art, with his keen eye for a deal, could see the possibilities of that company's healthy treasury. He could see these, even though the second payment in compensation for the cancellation of our ore contract had not yet been received.

At any rate, Art agreed to buy not only control of Abino from me, but control of the whole of ViolaMac. We closed the deal formally in July of 1960. Art's company, New Dickenson Mines, as it was then, paid George and me a little over $1.8 million for almost 1.5 million of our ViolaMac shares — most of them owned by me, of course, which amounted to 42% of ViolaMac's issued capital — and was enough to give Art control of what had always till then been my company.

Art White had been a well-known figure on Bay Street ever since he had managed to develop a group of Red Lake claims into the Dickenson mine toward the end of World War II. But there are those who still say today that the deal he made with me for ViolaMac really set the seal on his success.

This is my story, not Art White's, so I won't even try to explain all the complicated corporate developments that followed our deal except in the barest outline. Very soon after we closed the deal, Art amalgamated Lake Cinch with his New Dickenson Mines to form a company renamed just Dickenson Mines, and I was told the amalgamation had important tax advantages for Dickenson.

ViolaMac continued to run the Kam-Kotia mine as a subsidiary until 1966, when Art had a reorganization, dropped the ViolaMac name, and continued the operation under the name of Kam-Kotia Mines Ltd. And the Kam-Kotia worked out very well for him. Building on the work we had already done, he got our mill into production in 1961, and that year the mine produced copper and zinc worth $1.4 million. Production rose steadily until in 1969 it peaked at $15.8 million. Then there was a steep decline, and the mine was closed at the end of 1972. During its lifetime, the mine I bought for less than $200,000 produced copper and zinc, and a little gold and silver, worth altogether almost $80 million.

As we had feared, the Victor was almost played out by the time we sold it. Art discontinued its operation in 1962, leased it to independent operators for I think three more years, but then it closed, and as far as I know it has never reopened. During the time I had it, the Victor produced well over nine million dollars' worth of ore. But in the years it struggled on after I sold it I don't think it produced much more than about a quarter of a million dollars' worth.

Art was unlucky with the Abino, too. There was gold there, all right, but after spending more than half a million dollars on exploration hoping to repeat his success with the Dickenson, Art decided it was too scattered to make a profitable mine and discontinued operations. I heard recently, though, that someone is still working on it, so who knows, maybe the Abino will one day go into production. Stranger things have happened in the mining business. [The Abino mine produced a small amount of gold, about 1,400 ounces, between 1985–'86.]

When I negotiated my deal with Art White, I kept some of my ViolaMac shares for old time's sake, and I stayed on as vice-president of the new company. But I was accustomed to running my own show, and after about a year I decided to go out on my own again.

I had always had a soft spot in my heart for the old "Arrow," Consolidated Golden Arrow Mines Ltd., to give it its full name as it was then. This was one of the companies that had gone over to Art White with ViolaMac, but when I told Art I wanted out, he agreed to sell back enough shares of Arrow to give me control of it again.

I was very grateful to him. After all, the Arrow was one of the very first companies I had ever been associated with, back in Timmins long before the war. Also, it still had a substantial interest in the old Slocan Rambler, and even though we had never been able to reopen that property, I was pleased that I would still have a link, however slight, with the New Denver area where I had spent so many happy times. And just in case I was finally able to make a go of the Arrow, I guess, Art maintained a minority interest in it. If I recall correctly, it amounted to about 37%.

In another deal just before I took sick, I had had the Arrow buy a gold prospect consisting of 13 claims in the Dogpaw Lake area of the Kenora District, in northwest Ontario. And as soon as I regained control of the company I made arrangements for a diamond-drilling program to explore those claims.

I suppose I knew I was going against my doctor's orders, but it felt great to be back in business again. I still had several companies that had always been outside ViolaMac, and so had not been included in the sale to Art White, such as MacMillan Prospecting, Variometer Surveys, Airquests, and a few more. And oh, how often I have wished through all the years that have passed since then that I had been content with this modest "empire," and had not tried to expand beyond it — because it was the next company I acquired that involved me, and I still insist it was through no fault of my own, in a scandal so dreadful that even a quarter of a century later I can't think about it without shuddering.

The Windfall Affair, they called it. It was in the headlines for months in the mid-'60s. You just couldn't get away from it. And the stories that went with those headlines were as often as not written by reporters who didn't seem to understand the first thing about the events they were writing about. Things that were accepted practice in the mining business, and had been done that way since time began, were described as though they were at least immoral, if not downright criminal.

I never did find out much about the early history of the company I now wish I had never heard of, except that it was incorporated in 1946 as Windward Gold Mines Ltd., with some claims in the Kenora District. The company was reorganized in 1957. Its name was changed to Windfall Oils & Mines Ltd., and shortly afterwards its control passed to an American company, Sterling Oil of Oklahoma Inc. At that time Sterling intended to use it to branch out into the oil and gas business in Canada. But apparently its efforts in that regard were unsuccessful, because George and I were able to buy control of Windfall in December 1961, for about $65,000, and George became its president.

George had become interested in various U.S. mining areas when we were out looking for uranium prospects in the early '50s, and one of our first ventures with Windfall was to secure options on a couple of former copper-producing properties in Nevada, where we commissioned some geophysical exploration, after which Dr. Ambrose recommended a drilling program.

Before this got properly under way, though, our interest returned to our old stamping ground of the Porcupine with a vengeance. In the spring of 1964 a U.S. company, Texas Gulf Sulpher, announced a major strike of zinc, copper, and silver near Timmins which eventually became Kidd Creek, the single largest base metal mine in the world.

That announcement sparked a whirlwind of activity in the Timmins area, and on the Toronto Stock Exchange. On April 17, the day after Texas Gulf disclosed its find, more than 30 million shares changed hands in Toronto, an all-time record for one day's trading. Investors clamoured to buy stock in all sorts of companies they had never heard of, just so long as they had ground somewhere around the Texas Gulf discovery. They were all hoping, of course, that the rich Texas Gulf ore body would carry on underground to their own properties.

I was caught up in the general excitement naturally, and I headed for Timmins with a big advantage over most other investors because one of my good friends was probably the most knowledgeable prospector in that area. John Larche had left school at the age of 15 to work on a diamond-drilling crew, and he learned his trade so well that he was offered a job underground when he was still too young to qualify for it under the provincial regulations. The money was good though, so young John faked his age and took the job. And in 1955, when he went into prospecting and independent contracting for himself, he had already built up a store of experience many much older men could not offer.

John knew the Timmins area like the back of his hand, and the rumours had been flying around there for months before Texas Gulf finally made its sensational announcement. By that time, John and his partner, Fred Rousseau, had assembled several parcels of claims in the area. They had also joined forces with another prospector, Don McKinnon, who had been a timber cruiser in the area of the Texas Gulf find.

I had helped John when he was getting started on his own and had employed him on several exploration jobs for ViolaMac. I found him in a room at the Empire Hotel in Timmins, where he and his partners had set up shop to deal with all the high flyers trying to buy their claims. He showed me maps and described the various properties they had to sell, but the one particular area that interested me on one of the maps John said he wasn't free to deal in. This parcel consisted of three separate groups of four claims each, about three miles from the Texas Gulf discovery, and what made them particularly interesting was that one of the groups of four claims, in Prosser Township, had been left out of the Texas Gulf staking by mistake.

I asked John why he wasn't free to negotiate with me on that parcel, and he said he had come to a tentative deal for those claims with Noranda. He was trying to make a million-dollar deal for himself and his partners: $100,000 down, with the balance of $900,000 payable a year later if Noranda took up the option.

I agreed with John that this parcel looked like the best prospect in the entire area around the Texas Gulf find, and told him he was entitled to a quick reply from Noranda. Either they would buy or they wouldn't. But they had no right to stall him when he had plenty of other buyers willing to move, including me!

I kept at John, and told him I wasn't going to budge from that hotel room until he had got an answer from Noranda. So, out of loyalty to me I'm sure, he called the Noranda field man he had been dealing with. This fellow said head office had still not made up its mind, but he would get onto them again right away.

Well, I just sat on and on in that room and it must have been near midnight when the phone rang and the Noranda field man said his head office had decided against the deal. Only then did John feel free to deal with me. So we got down to bargaining, and we eventually agreed that I should give John and his partners $100,000 cash right there, and 250,000 of my own shares of Windfall to be divided among them as they saw fit. They knew I planned to offer the properties to Windfall.

Immediately on my return to Toronto, I offered the properties to the directors of Windfall, as agreed with John and his partners, and eventually, in an arrangement approved at a special meeting of shareholders, they were transferred to the company in return for what I had paid for them, plus an option on 200,000 shares at 58 cents, exercisable within five years, and a 5% royalty on any ore ultimately produced from the properties. I thought this was a fair return for my success in securing the properties, in the face of heavy competition for any ground within miles of the Texas Gulf strike. So, apparently, did the Toronto Stock Exchange, which approved the deal before it was offered to the Windfall shareholders.

The newspapers called the Kidd Creek find the "Whirlybird discovery" because it developed out of an airborne electromagnetic survey of the Porcupine area. That same airborne survey had also detected a strong electromagnetic anomaly on the four Prosser Township claims that had been mistakenly left out of the Texas Gulf staking. This suggested that their geological structure might be a continuation of the one that had proved so rich at Kidd Creek. At any rate, that was the theory, so as soon as the property had been acquired by the company, a ground geophysical survey was commissioned to follow up the aerial work. This confirmed that the anomaly was one of the strongest known in the area, and as a result, a program of diamond drilling was begun early in July.

The drill had hardly begun to penetrate the ground when suddenly on July 6, and for some reason no one knows to this day, the price of Windfall shares began to skyrocket. They had closed the previous day at 56 cents. In the furious trading on July 6 they reached a high of more than two dollars.

It was the beginning of a nightmare that lasted through the rest of that month for all of us on the Windfall board, and would not end for George and me until almost five years later.

CHAPTER
SEVENTEEN

Long before I had gone to Timmins looking for some property in the Kidd Creek area, Windfall had been expanding its activities. As well as its exploration operations in Nevada, it had acquired a group of claims in Tiblemont Township, Quebec, and a 36-claim block which seemed to be well placed in Loveland Township, not far from the Kam-Kotia mine, which was by now producing handsomely for Art White.

This activity had naturally created a need for funds in the Windfall treasury, and two of the companies I controlled, Variometer Surveys and Golden Shaft Mines Ltd., had entered into an underwriting agreement with Windfall. This called for the immediate injection of $40,000 cash into the Windfall treasury through the purchase of 100,000 shares at 40 cents each and the purchase of a further 900,000 shares at three-month intervals, at prices ranging upwards from 40 to 70 cents.

The first problem that the sudden rise in the price of Windfall shares caused me arose out of a stock exchange regulation that said whenever the share price rose to double the price at which you had an option, whatever money you had agreed to pay for the optioned shares became "due and payable" into the company's treasury right away. So, long before the close of trading on that horrible day, July 6, I had a call from the exchange authorities ordering me to pay all the money I had undertaken to pay for the options into the Windfall treasury within the hour.

In all, that meant I had to find well over $400,000 immediately. Well, I didn't have that much spare cash on hand, so I had to dash over to my bank to negotiate a personal loan of $200,000 which, fortunately because my credit was good, I was able to do. With that, and the proceeds of selling some of the optioned shares on the market, I was able to meet my commitments. Those shares that I was forced to sell by the exchange's own regulations were the only ones I put on the market throughout the whole panic, and to the best of my knowledge, none of the other Windfall directors sold any of their shares either.

At one time we thought we might be able to dampen the frantic demand for the shares, and prevent the price from rising so crazily, by putting a large number of shares on the market from the treasury. But our solicitors informed us that the exchange's regulations did not permit us to do that. And so the price continued to rocket upwards.

After it was all over, the complaint made against George and me was that we had permitted the trading frenzy to develop, and maybe even encouraged it, by deliberately withholding the results of the assay on the drill core of that first hole on the Prosser Township property. That was ridiculous, because we were only following the normal accepted practice in the industry and waiting to send the core out for assay until the hole was completed to its planned depth.

On July 7, the day after the share prices started to take off, there was an emergency meeting of Windfall's board of directors. Afterwards, George, as president, issued a statement saying the only thing he could have said at that time was that the drill had entered a "mineralized graphitic shear" at the 416-foot level. This did not, of course, mean that Windfall had made any kind of valuable discovery. No one, not even the world's greatest experts, could tell at that stage. But still the share price headed up.

Perhaps the fact that the Windfall treasury had just been bolstered by all that money paid in for the options taken up by my companies, at the express orders of the stock exchange authorities, contributed to the speculation. At any rate, the thing just got wilder and wilder, and we now began to hear reports from the drilling company that its crew was being besieged by snoopers trying to find out what was in that drill core. I was told that one fellow even returned to the site three times in one day, each time trying to disguise himself by changing his clothes in the bush.

On July 10, Tom Cole, Windfall's secretary and a director of the company, received a telegram from the Toronto Stock Exchange demanding an explanation for the situation which had arisen, which was of course as much a mystery to us as to them. He replied giving the only hard information we had at that time, as contained in George's original statement, but added that we had now come to realize what was necessary before we continued drilling. We had not yet had a core shack built to protect the sections of the core from prying eyes as they were retrieved from the ground, and on July 7, the same day George made his first statement, we had ordered one built.

Tom Cole added to his letter to the exchange authorities a telegram we had received from the drilling company, which I think is worth quoting in full here:

> Diamond drill core building about half completed. Expect to be finished by next Monday night. Your bunkhouse should be finished by next Wednesday. Our men having trouble keeping snoopers from trying to get information off the property. We will be ready to continue drilling as soon as the camps are finished. Weather very hot.
>
> Bradley Bros.
>
> Timmins, Ont.

On July 14, while my head was in a complete whirl, and I just couldn't understand what on earth was going on, there was a meeting at the offices of the Ontario Securities Commission, which George and I and Tom Cole were ordered to attend. The others present, though I can't remember all their names now, included two members of the Commission, the chairman of the board of governors of the Toronto Stock Exchange, and its president and vice-president. It was a very high-level meeting, and it could have been very intimidating, except that the rest of those present were just as mystified as we were as to what was happening to the price of Windfall shares.

As the meeting progressed, we had a very thorough discussion about the procedure to be adopted concerning the rest of the drilling, the handling of the results once the hole was completed, and the influence press coverage was having on the market.

I want to emphasize here a fact that seemed to get overlooked later: the representatives of the Ontario Securities Commission and the Toronto Stock Exchange all agreed that it was proper procedure not to have assays made and published before the hole was completed. After all, if we had announced that there was nothing in the core and then a few hundred feet deeper into the ground the drill had struck rich ore, the fat would really have been in the fire.

But I do think a big mistake was made at that meeting. George was ordered to put the core under guard until all of it had been assayed. The air of mystery this created when the news became known sent the share prices even wilder. At one point they reached a high of $5.60. Someone must have been trying to manipulate the stock, though not anyone connected with Windfall, because along the way telegrams were sent to Toronto newspapers from New York, supposedly signed by George, who was in Timmins at the time. Those telegrams contained false assay results, at a time when the core had not yet been sent out for assay.

The realization later that the telegrams were bogus caused a break in the share price, but it was still above three dollars when we received the results of the assay of the completed hole on July 30. They were disastrous. After the exchange closed for the day, George had to announce that while some copper mineralization had been encountered in the core, the values were less than half a percent. In other words, no commercial values had been encountered.

It was tragic. The stock opened next day at only 80 cents, and closed for the day at $1.04. We were just devastated, and of course the howls went up for somebody's hide.

The Ontario government responded a couple of weeks later by announcing the appointment of Mr. Justice Arthur Kelly, a member of the Ontario Court of Appeal, as a one-man Royal Commission to investigate what had now become "the Windfall Affair."

The Commission sat for weeks in the spring of 1965 and heard dozens of witnesses, including of course, George and me. And when Mr. Justice Kelly handed down his report in the fall, George and I were shocked that he seemed to think we had been guilty of fraud, and the fact that he also strongly criticized the Ontario Securities Commission and the Toronto Stock Exchange did nothing to ease our pain.

Our world just fell apart over the next few years. Soon after the report was published, in the fall of 1965, George and I were charged with two counts of fraud. Many people have told me since that if the authorities had had as strong a case against us as they seemed to think they did, they would have had our cases tried long before they actually did, because the sad fact is that the court proceedings against us did not begin until November 1968, three full years later.

We pleaded not guilty, of course, but the cloud we were under during all that time was absolutely unbearable. I thought I would go mad. As soon as the Royal Commission was announced, I decided it was only fair to offer my resignation as president of the Prospectors and Developers Association. I didn't want that fine organization, of which I was so proud, to be under any sort of suspicion just because of my connection with it. My resignation was accepted, but the association was thrown into so much confusion that for the first time in its history it held no annual convention the following year, 1965.

Being in limbo so to speak, George and I did very little in a business way during the years we were awaiting trial. In fact, we spent most of our time more or less in retirement at another farm we had bought in West Gwillimbury Township, not far from Newmarket, a short drive north of Toronto.

Our trial, when it finally arrived, lasted almost two months. Judge Deyman, who was presiding over it, had an unfortunate accident and broke his collarbone, so that the Christmas recess was longer than we had anticipated. Finally, though, early in February 1969, Judge Deyman acquitted us on both charges. He ruled that throughout the whole thing we had said nothing to the press that could have accounted for the rise in Windfall shares, and had acted quite correctly and in accordance with accepted practice in not releasing the results of the assay until the hole had been completed. So we had committed no fraud.

The nightmare was over at last. I was so relieved for poor George, but the verdict was not much consolation to me because by that time I had already spent time in prison on another charge, which to this day many of my friends are convinced would never have been brought against me if it had not been for that cursed Windfall affair.

The details of that are quite simple. Ever since I had regained control of Consolidated Golden Arrow, George had been after me to sell him some shares in the company. As I said earlier in this book, we always kept our business affairs separate. I finally agreed to let him buy a block of 200,000 Arrow shares held by MacMillan Prospecting, which was entirely my own company. George was never a member of its board and didn't even hold any of its shares, so I saw nothing wrong with the transaction. But I told George, as I had always been led to believe, that since Arrow was a listed company on the Toronto Stock Exchange, I couldn't sell the shares to him privately. The deal would have to go through a broker and be reported on the stock exchange ticker like any other trade.

George, who always hated anything that sounded to him like red tape, grumbled a bit but finally agreed that if that was the way things had to be done, that was the way we'd have to do it. So I called a prominent stockbroker I often dealt with, Robert J. Breckenridge.

He was very well-known and at one time had been head of the Toronto Stock Exchange. I asked him to handle the transaction. The deal went through in one day but, probably because it was such a large block, it apparently created some interest among speculators, because Arrow shares which sold for 25 cents in the morning closed the day at 65 cents.

And in March 1967, I was convicted of "wash trading," which is usually described as creating a false or misleading appearance of active public trading in a stock. I couldn't believe my ears when I heard the judge sentence me to what they called an "indeterminate sentence not to exceed nine months in reformatory," and a fine of $10,000. Of course, I told my lawyer, Joe Sedgwick, to appeal.

But in January 1968 my appeal was denied. My cousin Elmer, the one I introduced to Annie — the girl he married when she replaced me as a maid at the Rodds' all those years before in Windsor — was having his dinner when he heard I would have to go to prison. He got up, walked to his room, and fell dead of a heart attack at the door.

The newspapers pointed out at the time that I was the only person ever sent to prison in Ontario for wash trading, and the oldest woman ever sent to reformatory. And the funny thing about that whole episode was that Mr. Breckenridge, whose firm put through the trade for me, was also charged with the same offence I was, yet he was found not guilty.

Many people have said to me over the years that I got a dirty deal, that I was just a scapegoat, and that if whatever I did was wrong, then a whole lot of other Bay Street people should have been put behind bars. That's not the point. I didn't feel guilty then, and I don't feel guilty now. But ever since I was a little girl, I have always been good at doing what I had to do. So even before the police came for me, I had made up my mind that, if this is what I have to do, okay, I'll do it. There may be a lesson in it for somebody else. And I'll live through it.

The two policemen who came for me when my appeal was turned down were very nice and apologetic. It was a bitterly cold day, and I had on the little fur jacket that George had bought me to go to the Coronation. When I was getting into the wagon the policemen, who apparently knew who I was, said they were very sorry and that I was one person they didn't want to take where they were going to take me, which was to the Don Jail.

I never come across a story about the Don Jail in the newspapers these days without shuddering, but the female staff there were very nice to me when I arrived. You have to give up your own things when you go into jail, and George took my fur jacket home for me. Also, I had heard somewhere that new arrivals in jail had to be stripped and deloused, so I steeled myself and said, "Okay, if you have to spray me, go ahead." But one of the female warders said, "Oh no, we don't have to spray you. You're Viola MacMillan." I can still hear her voice now. It made me very pleased.

I only had one bad night, really. That first night in the Don Jail. And yet, it's funny. I felt kind of relieved when the gate of my cell was locked behind me. At least I was alone in my own little sleeping place. There was a bad snowstorm outside, and I looked out the tiny window and thought, "Well, Viola, be thankful for small mercies. The worst has happened, but you're still alive and well, and you've just got to see it through."

CHAPTER
EIGHTEEN

I was only in the Don Jail for two or three days before they moved me to the Ingleside Women's Guidance Centre at Brampton, to serve the rest of my sentence. That was a much different place, just like a motel, really, and a lot more comfortable than some of the places I lived in when I was on the trail prospecting.

We were encouraged to choose various things to do for recreation, and a lot of the women chose sewing or painting. I chose to do something I was familiar with from my young days, typing. I would sit there day after day typing bits of my life story. That kept me going, thinking of all the things I had done in the past. The people who read my notes thought they were wonderful, but I would rip them all up next morning and then start over again. I wish I had kept those notes. They would have been useful to me in writing this book.

We were permitted to have visitors, thank goodness, and George came to see me as often as he was allowed to. Other friends came as well, much to my relief. I wasn't kept in chains or anything, but being cooped up like that was terribly frustrating when I had always been so active.

I was overjoyed when, after about nine weeks, I was told the authorities had reviewed my case and I was to be released on parole the next day. I don't know whether it was my advanced age, or they were worried about my health, or what, but at six o'clock the next morning they came for me and drove me to Toronto, where George was waiting for me at a friend's house. We had a lovely breakfast there, and I wish I could say it was a very joyous occasion and all our troubles were behind us, but of course we still had to face those fraud charges, and we still had no idea when the authorities would be ready to proceed with our case. Even though we were convinced we had done no wrong, how could we be sure the judge would agree with us? That long period of suspense was just horrible, and I still think it was unforgivable.

At any rate, we continued to spend most of our time at our West Gwillimbury farm. There was, of course, still a certain amount of routine business that had to be attended to from time to time with our companies, but we didn't even try to plan any new ventures during this period. It wasn't until after we had been acquitted of all charges and the whole nasty business was behind us that we felt we could begin to live a normal life again.

Throughout the late 1960s, Windfall continued to do exploration work on its properties in Nevada and in northern Ontario. In 1969, the company took an option on 40 uranium claims in Clarendon Township, near Bancroft, in Eastern Ontario, which was a new area of operations for us. I took an option on 36 adjacent claims on behalf of Consolidated Golden Arrow, and the two companies collaborated in some preliminary exploration work. Unfortunately, our efforts were unsuccessful and we surrendered the claims in 1970, at around the same time as I secured the shareholders' agreement to change the name of the latter company to the simpler Canadian Arrow Mines Ltd.

Perhaps this last chapter of my book would have been different if George and I had made one more big strike, but alas we never did, and during the '70s we gradually wound down our business activities. After all, we were both well past the usual retirement age, and on the plus side, the slower pace gave us more leisure time to spend at the farm, which we both loved, and on our winter vacations in Florida, where in our heyday we owned a lovely apartment.

One of our most interesting ventures in those years developed purely by accident when we were driving down to Florida with my brother Ed in the fall of 1976. We got up at the motel one morning and heard on the television that Jimmy Carter had been elected President the night before. I could tell from our road atlas that our motel was only about 90 miles south of Plains, Georgia, which was Carter's hometown, of course. On impulse I said to George, "Let's go back and see if we can meet him." I had been reading one of Carter's books and thought he was a great fellow, and as a farm girl myself, I liked the idea of a farm boy being able to become President of the United States.

George was all for the idea, so we drove back north, found Plains, and as luck would have it, Jimmy Carter was speaking from the railroad platform there. We both liked him and the sincere way he spoke and George said, "Let's buy some property here." So we made some inquiries and didn't we find that "the old Carter place" was up for sale. It was an old frame house, which was where Jimmy's grandmother lived when she settled in Plains years before with her family, including Jimmy's father. It seemed that the old man who owned the place when we arrived there — I guess he must have been a Republican — didn't like Jimmy and wanted to sell and get out.

The house had about an acre of ground around it, with nice trees, and George decided to buy it. I wasn't fussy about buying it at all because it was not much of a house, and not in very good shape. But then we had an idea. We could spend some money restoring it, charge a small admission fee to the tourists who would flock to see it as a historical landmark, and when we had recovered our outlay, present it to the citizens of the town as a gesture of friendship between Canada and the United States.

So that is what we did. We formed a corporation to undertake the job, and even bought another, much nicer, house to live in while we supervised the restoration work. This was a doctor's house: a lovely, two-storey place right across the road from the one belonging to Jimmy's famous mother, "Miss Lillian," and where he has his office now.

I guess we spent about $100,000 restoring that old house, and I did a lot of the work myself, stripping paper off the walls, taking up old floor coverings, and things like that. I enjoyed it though.

I found some old snapshots of Jimmy's grandmother and his father, and one of his uncles who later had a store in Plains. I had paintings done from them, which I hung in the house in lovely frames. And when we finally opened for visitors, it was with pretty curtains on the windows that I had sewn myself.

And the tourists really did pour through that place. I swear the cars used to begin arriving as early as six o'clock in the morning. We got to know Plains quite well, and met Jimmy Carter. We went to the same church he went to, where he also taught Sunday school. And to this day, anyone who visits Plains can go through that house and see the antiques we put there, and those paintings of Jimmy's family. I disposed of the house to the local Methodist church a couple of years ago, and we had sold the doctor's house long before then.

That project in Plains, so different from our early days in our canoes and tents in the bush, yet quite an adventure in its own way, was the last one George and I ever shared. One morning in September 1978, up at the farm, he got out of bed and went into the bathroom right next to where we were sleeping. I always was a light sleeper and I heard him go. I remember it vividly even now. It was five minutes to five, awfully early for George to be up and about. He had not been feeling too well for a few weeks and I had begun to worry about him, so I jumped out of bed too and rushed to the bathroom door.

"Are you all right, George?" I called in.

He didn't reply, except when he came out of the bathroom he said, "I'm not going back to bed." I sat him down in a comfortable old chair we had in our bedroom. There was something about his appearance that frightened me and I told him, "Now George, you stay right there and I'll run and get Flora." That was his sister, who was staying with us and was asleep in the big bedroom upstairs. We were down on the main floor.

John, the man who looked after the farm for us, was with us

for 22 years, and slept across the hall from the main bedroom upstairs. After rousing Flora, I banged on his door and told him George was not well and to come downstairs fast. And by the time I got back into the room from calling the hospital to send an ambulance, John was putting George's shoes on for him.

Flora was there too, and George said, "Can you fan me Flora?" So his sister picked up a magazine and began to fan him. I just put a blanket over him to keep him warm and then stood beside his chair with my hand on his shoulder. Poor George. He just looked up at me and his eyes sort of flickered and suddenly he was dead.

It was all over as quick as that. At least he didn't have to suffer at the end, as so many people do. I give thanks for that, and for the many, many happy years we had together. We seldom had any cross words and I never once regretted marrying George.

In the early days, when I took on running the Prospectors and Developers Association, some of the prospectors' wives used to become suspicious when they heard their husbands singing my praises. But I used to tell them, "You don't have to worry about me. I have my man, and he's wonderful."

And he was wonderful, as all the tributes to him said after his death. Everyone loved George, he was so friendly and easygoing. And everyone was very kind to me in my loss. A particular tower of strength to me then, and in the years since, was a neighbour of ours in the country, Franc Joubin. Franc's beloved wife Mary — I knew her better than Franc at the time — had died a few months before George, so Franc knew what I was going through.

I knew him in a professional way too, of course, because the name Franc Joubin will always stand high in the annals of Canadian mining history. He is one of the most brilliant geologists this country has ever produced and among his many discoveries were the huge uranium deposits that made the town of Elliot Lake famous around the world. After that discovery made him a millionaire, Franc went on to devote the rest of his life to helping underdeveloped countries through the United Nations. I am proud to say that we are still very good friends.

That year, 1978, which will always be a sad one in my memory, ended on a happier note. A few weeks after George's death, I received a very official-looking letter from Ottawa. It contained a full pardon for the offence of which I had been convicted and which had resulted in me going to jail. Oh, how I wished that document had arrived a couple of months earlier while George was still alive. It would have been such a consolation to him.

Then, just before Christmas I received another official letter, this time from the executive director of the Canadian Institute of Mining and Metallurgy, the organization that had refused to accept me as a member during the war because I was a woman. "It is my privilege and pleasure," this letter began, "to advise you that, in view of your long service to the Institute and the Mineral Industry, it was unanimously resolved at a Meeting of Council on October 13, 1978, you be designated a Life Member of the Institute effective January 1st, 1979." So, if you wait long enough, the world eventually catches up with you.

As for whatever breach there had been between me and the association that I so loved and to which I had devoted so much of my life, the Prospectors and Developers, that had long since been healed. I no longer took an active part in its direction, but as a life member and former president, I was always made welcome at its annual conventions. It was one of the high points of my year to meet old friends there, and hear first-hand about all the exciting new developments in the mining industry.

As for my own involvement in that industry, I was starting to realize — reluctantly, I must admit — that the time had come for me to pass on the torch to younger hands, and begin to disengage myself from my various business involvements. It was not an easy decision to make, believe me, but as I've said earlier in this book, once I knew I had to do something, I was able to buckle down and do it.

In 1979, I sold my control of Windfall Oils and Mines to a company whose board of directors included several principals of Goldlund Mines, which at that time had a promising property adjoining some Windfall claims in Echo Township in Northern Ontario. I gather the company later changed hands again, as is often the way in the mining business, but I'm afraid I didn't follow its activities after I severed my relationship with it, so I don't know whether any gold was ever found on those claims, or might be in the future.

Then there was Canadian Arrow, the company I had owned, with other shareholders of course, ever since my early days in Timmins before the war. I had never lost faith in those Hislop Township claims I had bought from dear old Mayor Bartleman and his partners. The rock brought up from the shaft George and I had sunk, and the cross-cuts we had pushed out from it underground, contained gold, I was sure of it. But that was in the old days, when the price of gold was still fixed at $35 to the ounce, and there was just not enough gold there at that price to make a mine. But now, gold could be sold at whatever price buyers all over the world were prepared to pay for it. And at one time that price reached more than $800 an ounce.

In these new circumstances, the big mining companies had started to become interested in lots of prospects that had just been completely uneconomical in the old days. So in 1980, I was able to negotiate a deal on behalf of Canadian Arrow with Pamour Porcupine Mines — the very same company whose interest in the Quartet Syndicate ground so long ago had led to my first big break: my deal that resulted in the Hallnor mine.

Pamour had for some time been running a custom smelter in Timmins, which was processing gold ore from a number of small mining companies. In fact, it had signed a deal with Canadian Arrow a few years earlier under which it had milled several thousand tons of the rock excavated in Arrow's earlier operations. I forget now how much gold they extracted, but the Canadian Arrow treasury did receive some payments until the price of gold slipped on the world market, and Pamour suspended work.

They did not lose interest in the property though, and in 1980 I sold Pamour enough of my shares to give that company effective control of Canadian Arrow. I negotiated a 20-year lease arrangement, under which Arrow stood to receive a 30% royalty on the net profits of any ore mined from those six claims in Hislop Township. Pamour then began to operate an open-pit operation, and if my memory serves me correctly, the Arrow treasury benefited to the extent of something over $300,000 before the price of gold on the world market dropped again, and work was suspended in 1982.

The Canadian Arrow story is not yet over, however. Nor is my involvement with that company. In 1988, Pamour sold its interest in Arrow to a Toronto investment banking company owned, I believe, by a couple of Australian entrepreneurs. By that time, even though I still held a considerable number of Arrow shares, I could at best be described as only a bystander, and knew little or nothing about the company's affairs.

But toward the end of 1989, I was delighted to learn that control of Arrow had been bought by none other than my dear friend from Timmins, John Larche. And if anyone can develop those Hislop Township claims into a successful producing mine, and realize the hopes George and I had for them going back to those days before the war, I'm sure John Larche is that man.

I am nearing the end of my story now, but I should mention one more what you might call "corporate development" that took place early in 1989. It did not, and will not, make any waves on Bay Street, but it was a great satisfaction to me from a sentimental point of view.

For quite some time, my lawyer, Tom Cole, who took over from Kelso Roberts more years ago than either of us cares to remember, had been urging me to sort of tidy up, to simplify my affairs. So I consolidated two of my remaining companies, Variometer Surveys and MacMillan Prospecting, into a third company which has not so far come into this story, for a quite natural reason.

Lucky Texas was a company I set up at the time of the Kidd Creek discovery when, along with a lot of other people, I hoped to acquire some property nearby that would enable me to share in the Texas Gulf bonanza. As you have read, Kidd Creek was not exactly lucky for me, and I never activated Lucky Texas.

So I was quite happy to agree when Mr. Cole suggested that I merge Variometer Surveys and MacMillan Prospecting into Lucky Texas, because I already had a new name, or rather an old name of which I was very fond, to give to the new corporate structure. I am now the president and only shareholder of a private company, ViolaMac Limited. I was able to revive the name because Art White surrendered it when he merged my original company into his Kam-Kotia company.

It was in 1989, too, as I was nearing the end of compiling this story of my life, that an opportunity arose out of the blue for me to repay my native land, which has been so good to me. One day my friend Dorothy Ginn — she was president of the Women's Association of the Mining Industry of Canada and her husband had my old post as president of the Prospectors and Developers Association — invited me to lunch. But on the way she wanted to drop in at the offices of the big mining company, Teck. I had no idea why.

Once there, we were ushered into the office of Teck's president, Dr. Norman Keevil Jr. He took the opportunity to tell me about a project that he was involved in as a trustee of a special committee, working for the National Museum of Natural Sciences in Ottawa. This project, he explained, was raising $5 million to purchase for Canada one of the greatest collections of minerals in the world, which had been accumulated by an American collector named William Pinch who lived in Rochester, New York.

This was the first I had heard about this project, but by a strange coincidence, I had seen a small portion of the collection, which had been one of the exhibits at the P.D.A. convention in the Royal York Hotel in March 1989. I had been overwhelmed by the magnificence of those minerals, just as they had come from the ground, but all beautifully lit in their glass cases. Some of them, I didn't even know their names. But I kept buttonholing my friends and telling them not to miss the exhibit. Now Mr. Keevil came to the point. The trustees, mining people, and others with just an amateur interest in gem stones and minerals generally, had secured some quite handsome donations from mining companies. But they were still a long way short of achieving their objective of meeting the full purchase price of the collection. So they had decided to approach individuals they thought might have an interest in making sure that this collection would be a permanent asset to Canada. So how about me?

Naturally, I asked for time to think it over. I knew I would make some sort of donation, of course, but how much? In the days that followed my mind went back over my past life. I remembered how as a little girl I used to listen entranced to my brother Joe's stories about his work in the silver mine at Cobalt. I recalled the happiness of my early days on the trail with George, and the comradeship of all the prospectors who had become our friends then and during the years I worked to represent their interests as the head of their association.

George and I never found a pot of gold at the foot of our rainbow, but our exertions gave us a full and satisfying life, and the security and independence we were eventually able to enjoy came from some of those other minerals that lie beneath the surface of this great land. Now George was gone. I had sold the Oriole Parkway house and the farm, and living in my Toronto apartment, my wants were very few.

After about three weeks I had made my decision, and I'm sure if George had still been alive he would have approved of it. I pledged $1.25 million to the campaign to buy the Pinch collection for Canada.

I was immediately invited to Ottawa, where I was made very welcome by Dr. Alan Emery, director of the National Museum of Natural Sciences which, I learned, grew out of the activities of the Geological Survey of Canada going back even before Confederation in 1867. Dr. Emery told me of the plans to house the collection in a special gallery of the museum. It would be in the very building of the Department of Mines in which I had pleaded for government help for my prospectors during World War II, to enable them to find the minerals we needed to win the war.

My donation, Dr. Emery told me, had put the campaign "over the top," and possession of the collection was now assured for Canada for all time. And in recognition, he said, the trustees proposed, with my agreement, to call it the Viola MacMillan National Mineral Exhibition Gallery.

Well, I was overwhelmed, of course, and told him they couldn't do that. But secretly, naturally I was flattered and very, very pleased. I thought back to those days after the war when I had tried so hard, and failed, to interest others in my proposal for a Mining Day to raise awareness among Canada's young people of the importance of the mining industry. I had not succeeded then, but perhaps now? So I did not play coy too long, and when the gallery opens in 1992 it will bear my name.

I still remember how impressed I was by the beauty of those exhibits I saw at the P.D.A. convention, and they were just a fraction of the total of 16,000 items in the Pinch collection. If the permanent display of all those wonderful treasures from the earth inspires future generations of Canadians to share my lifelong fascination with Canada's underground wealth, and recognize its importance to our country's prosperity, I shall rest content.

AFTERWORD

BY VIRGINIA HEFFERNAN
MARCH 2001

The name Viola MacMillan evokes one of two responses. Those who knew her personally describe a generous and dynamic professional who became the sacrificial lamb of a corrupt Bay Street. Those introduced to her by the press recall a scoundrel who swindled innocent investors out of their savings. Will the real Viola Rita MacMillan please stand up?

If MacMillan were alive today, she would readily rise and state her case, just as she did on the 1960s television program, *To Tell the Truth*. As her memoirs divulge, she was an aggressive personality who rose from humble beginnings to achieve success in the mining industry: Canada's own Horatio Alger, some would say. Despite her tiny stature — she stood just five feet tall and weighed little more than 100 pounds — she fought her way to the top of a man's world by sheer force of will and a refusal to take 'no' for an answer. "Anybody, regardless of sex or circumstance, can do anything they want to do. All you need is the guts to stick to things," was her favourite response to queries about the secret of her success.

But she rarely spoke of what became known as the Windfall Affair, a mining scandal in the 1960s that triggered a Royal Commission investigation, exposed weaknesses in the market regulatory system, and shamed several high-ranking officials. Even

MacMillan's otherwise detailed autobiography gives scant attention to an event that not only rocked her world, but changed the dynamics of share trading in Canada forever. MacMillan carried a long list of accomplishments to her grave, but her name will always be synonymous with Windfall.

MacMillan and the mining industry were joined at the hip. She spent her waking hours lobbying on the industry's behalf, organizing professional and social activities for miners and prospectors, combing the bush for signs of hidden mineral wealth, or nurturing her children: the bevy of junior mining companies that she ran with her husband, George. "If you want to see Viola, you've got to get up early and catch her on the run," George MacMillan told *Maclean's* magazine in 1957. The mining industry was the stage upon which MacMillan orchestrated some of her finest performances and, in return, she was the industry's most vocal advocate. Even their fortunes seemed in sync.

There was less balance in her marriage. Observers say Viola dominated while the happy-go-lucky George was content to take instruction from his more assertive wife. Their business alliance mirrored their personal relationship. Viola was the financial whiz and dealmaker who called the shots, George the technical expert who handled most of the hands-on fieldwork. "She took a lot of the glamour, but he was the prospector," remembers Mort Brown, former editor of *The Northern Miner*.

Judging from their success, they made a good team. Among the couple's mining coups were the discovery of the Hallnor gold mine in Ontario, and the development of the Victor lead-zinc (ViolaMac Mines) and Lake Cinch uranium deposits in British Columbia and Saskatchewan, respectively. "There are few mining camps that did not feel the tread of George's boots in the bush and the two as a team made a deep impression on the progress . . . of many (mining) areas," read George's 1978 obituary in *The Northern Miner*.

AFTERWORD

"LET ME CALL YOU SWEETHEART"

But before the Windfall Affair would cast a shadow over her public image, Viola MacMillan was best known for her leadership of the Prospectors and Developers Association (P.D.A.). (It was renamed the Prospectors and Developers Association of Canada (P.D.A.C.) in 1986.) Under her reign as president from 1944 until she resigned in 1964, the organization's membership grew from a handful to more than 4,000. The annual convention she organized at the Royal York Hotel in Toronto became *the* place to option properties, to discuss issues relevant to exploration, and — just as important to those who spent the remainder of the year in the bush — to party.

To this day, the P.D.A.'s March convention remains a colorful event where the booze flows freely, the dancing extends well past midnight, and promoters are granted three full days to shout from their soapboxes to a captive audience. The networking events coincide with technical talks and short courses given by some of the brightest in the business. Today's 6,000-plus attendees can thank MacMillan, so dedicated to the event that she would drive drunken prospectors home in the wee hours of the morning, for what has become the best-known mining gathering in the world. "She did a lot of arm-twisting to obtain high-quality speakers and other seminar leaders to participate and generally made the conventions happen," says her former accountant Robert Ford.

Winning over the heads and hearts of her fellow miners did not come easily. There were some P.D.A. members who resented the appointment of a female president, including the organization's founder, Walter Segsworth. But MacMillan gradually earned the respect of many of her peers. Eventually, her gender became a non-issue. "The great and not-so-great have ceased to wag their heads and wonder," reads a profile of MacMillan in *Men and Mines*, published in 1962. "They know Viola MacMillan is an outstanding pioneer of Canadian mining, who commands respect not because she is 'Mrs. President,' but because of her own achievement." To express gratitude to the tiny bundle of energy that was their leader, P.D.A. members would serenade MacMillan with a rendition of "Let Me Call You Sweetheart" whenever she stepped up to the podium. "The P.D.A. was her life," explains Robert Ginn, who followed in MacMillan's footsteps as P.D.A. president in 1989. "No one was willing or able to spend as much time on the organization as she did."

What was it like to be the only powerful woman in a man's world? This question fascinated the press, becoming the subject of many a magazine feature and column in the women's pages of daily newspapers throughout the 1940s and 1950s. MacMillan's membership in the mining fraternity earned her a file folder of nicknames, including "angel of the sourdoughs," "Queen Bee," and "sweetheart of the mining men." But she was too busy getting things done to ponder her unusual status. She was scornful of the feminist movement, believing a woman could be successful in any career with a little luck, a strong will, and lots of hard work. "I see no reason why girls can't take their places beside the men in the field," she said in a 1948 radio broadcast. "Mind you, they must expect to pull their weight and not be cry-babies when things don't go too well — when it rains and the fire goes out, or when the black flies make life miserable."

The "girls" may have taken their place beside the men in the bush, but they haven't advanced much further. The reins of power in the mining industry remain in male hands. Although working in the field is difficult for men with families, it is virtually out of the question for married women still taking the lion's share of domestic responsibility. University geology and mining engineering classes may have an equal proportion of men and women, but most female graduates eventually develop related careers in research, education, communications, or finance. They rarely make it to the executive ranks of the mining industry.

The most notable recent exception is Margaret (Peggy) Witte, the audacious promoter named Woman of the Year by *Chatelaine* magazine in 1994. A metallurgical engineer, Witte oversaw the rise and fall of Royal Oak Mines, a medium-sized gold producer with major-league aspirations. Before Royal Oak collapsed under the weight of high debt, low gold prices, and environmental liabilities, she successfully restructured three money-losing gold mines and launched a bold (but ultimately unsuccessful) takeover bid for one of Canada's top-tier companies, Lac Minerals.

Witte also made a lot of enemies. During a bitter, two-year strike at the company's Giant mine in The Northwest Territories, she hired scabs to keep the mine running, an unusual and provocative move in the mining business. The striking miners were outraged and took to calling her "Miss Piggy." Their fury culminated in an exploding bomb that killed nine people, including three replacement workers. A former Giant miner set the bomb, but the responsibility for the attack fell on Witte's shoulders. She later took the fall for Royal Oak's demise. Today, Witte is trying to rebuild her reputation as chairman and chief executive officer of Eden Roc Mineral Corp., a junior exploration company with properties in West Africa.

Inevitably, comparisons have been drawn between MacMillan and Witte. Both ignored their "female handicap" to become leaders in the mining industry. Both dominated in their marriages: MacMillan by taking the upper hand in her personal and business dealings with George; Witte by hiring her husband, Bill, who later walked out of the job and the marriage. Both enjoyed the trappings of their success: Witte gravitated towards private club memberships and yachts; MacMillan preferred fur coats and the latest Fifth Avenue fashions. Both acquired a high public profile, only to plunge into obscurity when their dreams faltered and their integrity was questioned. The main difference between the two was the degree of femininity. "Viola used her feminine guile in business. Witte was much more aggressive," says Ginn.

THE LURE OF THE LOTTERY

But if the character of mining's female leaders hasn't changed much, the industry has. Following World War II, North Americans were optimistic and ready to rebuild their lives and countries. Metals for new cars and infrastructure, and for the huge reconstruction taking place in Europe and Japan, were in demand. Canada was considered a vast reservoir of these metals and exploration from British Columbia to Nova Scotia took on new urgency.

By 1951 the value of Canadian mineral production hit a record $1.23 billion, more than double the figure a decade earlier. "I hope you will agree with me when I say we cannot avoid the conclusion that the leading place in the next half-century in the mineral world belongs to Canada," said MacMillan, then P.D.A. president, to the Colorado Mining Association in 1952.

Her comments would prove prophetic. By 1999, the mining industry was contributing more than $27 billion annually to the Canadian economy and had become the second largest earner of foreign exchange. Canada now ranks first in the production and export of potash and uranium, second in nickel, zinc, and cadmium, and third in aluminum and platinum group metals. Canada is also the mine financing capital of the world, where about 40% of the money for new mines originates. International mining companies, including Normandy Mining of Australia, have listed on the Toronto Stock Exchange (TSE) in order to take advantage of Canadian markets to finance the exploration and development of mineral deposits the world over.

There are three stages to building a mine. First, the ore deposit must be found through exploration. The second stage involves development, when the infrastructure and mine facilities are built based on economic, geological, and engineering parameters. Finally, the mine enters the production phase when ore is extracted, refined, and sold and the huge capital input required during the development stage is slowly repaid. It can take anywhere from three to six or more years for a mine to pay back upfront costs.

Exploration is the riskiest of the three stages. Only about one in 1,000 properties yields an encouraging discovery and about one in 100 discoveries develops into a mine. But the exploration stage can also be the most rewarding because the costs are relatively minor compared to the potential wealth generated by an economic find. This high-risk/high-reward scenario is a magnet for speculators who will readily invest in penny mining stocks in return for the slim chance of participating in a bonanza.

Indeed, the speculative money raised by junior mining companies on Canada's stock exchanges pays for exploration worldwide, with the exception of projects financed by producing companies through cash flow from their operations. After enjoying a spectacular run in the mid-1990s, junior mining stocks fell from grace when the Bre-X scandal erupted in 1997. But the speculative market activity was reincarnated in the high-tech boom that fueled market advances during the late 1990s, when just about everyone with money in the stock market participated in the technology sector. The risk-reward factor associated with exploration is akin to the risk of research and development in technology: they both carry a wide range of potential financial outcomes, including the chance to hit the jackpot.

After the war, all the ingredients were in place for a penny stock market explosion: a loosely regulated exchange that encouraged speculation; non-taxable capital gains; high metal prices; seemingly limitless demand for certain metals; and an optimistic public ready to take a gamble. "During the two decades immediately after the Second World War, a large section of the general public in Ontario purchased penny stocks at one time or another," wrote geologist Franc Joubin in his memoir, *Not for Gold Alone*. "Practically all forms of lotteries or games of chance were then illegal, save for official racetrack wagering and modest church- or charity-sponsored fundraising. The considerable inherent speculative instinct of the public responded enthusiastically to such penny stock involvement. In many circles, discussion of various penny stocks was often as common as discussion of the weather."

Though there were many more losers than winners, the postwar investment in exploration paid off. Prospectors relying on grubstakes from informal financing syndicates or speculative share companies discovered several significant deposits, including the Manitouwadge base metal mines in northern Ontario. Joubin, for instance, financed initial staking of what was to become the $30-billion Blind River uranium field in Ontario from a $15,000 "mad money" account set up by Toronto promoter Joe Hirshhorn to allow Joubin — who had a good nose for new mines — to act on his hunches. "Unquestionably, many of the great mines of Canada emerged through the use of penny-share financing," said Joubin.

Viola MacMillan was in the thick of the market action. She was already a veteran prospector who had made some serious money on the Hallnor gold mine. While Joubin was staking one of the biggest uranium deposits in the world, MacMillan was reaping the profits from her Victor lead-zinc-silver mine in British Columbia. (Unbeknownst to the two up-and-coming prospectors was that they would become best friends in their old age.) MacMillan reinvested the Victor returns in more than a dozen junior companies and joined the uranium rush that was taking shape across Canada. Meanwhile, she was winning respect for her decade-long leadership of the P.D.A., which hit the 1000-member mark in 1952. "I have never been happier, or busier, than I was in the 1950s," she remembers in these pages.

During these boom days for mining, exploration financing was handled by slick promoters who worked the city phones while their technical sidekicks scoured the bush for new deposits. If a promoter decided to take on a new prospect, he would form a public company and issue a few million shares, then split about a quarter of the issue with the prospector as a reward for taking the initial risks. In Toronto, these promoters were known as the "Bay St. Buccaneers" for their skills at wheeling, dealing, and risk-taking. They were the catalysts that brought together properties in the deep bush with cash from the big city. MacMillan was both promoter and prospector, as happy placing calls from her downtown penthouse as she was operating out of a tent in the bush. "She could make the time of day seem exciting," recalls Ford.

Promoters are as vital to exploration as marketers are to consumer products. They create a market for early-stage exploration opportunities that would otherwise remain untested. They fund the long-shot, the hole in the bush that will either hit the jackpot or, far more likely, come up barren. Their ability to spin a story and convince the public to invest in imaginative but risky ventures is the underpinning for new wealth creation in the mining industry.

But the greed inherent in penny stock speculation combined with loose regulations and enforcement establishes a fertile breeding ground for unscrupulous activity. That lethal combination was particularly evident in MacMillan's heyday. Petty crimes like wash trading, in which stock was bought and sold by the same company or individual to create the impression of strong market activity, were usually overlooked, just as jay walking might be today. "It was like the Wild West on the (Toronto) Stock Exchange," says Justice Patrick Hartt, who acted as counsel on the Royal Commission investigation into the Windfall Affair in 1965. "Wash trading was a common practice."

Outright fraud, in which a promoter would talk up a worthless property otherwise known as "moose pasture," then take profits when the stock appeared to be nearing its peak, was frowned upon but often left undetected or undisciplined. "In those days you could do anything. It was the norm," says Brown. The cardinal rule in stock promotion was never, ever marry your own deal. In other words, be prepared to bail out of a sinking ship before the passengers find out it's going down.

The regulatory bodies in Canada co-operated by looking the other way, either too understaffed or too timid to discipline the roguish elements of the penny stock community. "The Canadian markets were regarded, by and large, as just about as crooked as any game on earth by foreign investors," says Grant MacMillan, an insurance executive and distant relative of George MacMillan. "It was embarrassing to hear the government and the justice system being denounced because of rapacious crooks that showed up in Europe with valises full of worthless paper that would be laid off at great prices with many lies."

Ironically, in 1964 — just before the Windfall scandal broke — the TSE rules for mine listings were called too restrictive by prospectors, who felt their livelihood threatened from two sides: new geophysical technology that could pinpoint potential ore bodies, theoretically reducing the need for old-fashioned prospecting; and excessive market regulation. Members of the TSE were encouraged to take a more active role in raising initial financing for mining ventures. At that year's P.D.A. convention, 2000 prospectors and exchange officials met in Toronto for a panel discussion on whether exchange red tape was delaying financing for prospects. MacMillan — as usual — was at the centre of the fray, issuing threats about forming a junior stock exchange with easier listing requirements if the TSE didn't loosen up a little.

TEXAS GULF IGNITES A RUSH

But all the squabbling over listing and trading requirements was quickly forgotten in the excitement over a new discovery near Timmins, Ontario, which became the Kidd Creek mine, the richest base metal mine in the world. Rumours had been circulating since the beginning of the year that Texas Gulf Sulpher, an American company, was amassing large tracts of land in the Timmins area and flying unusual quantities of drill core out of the area by helicopter. In fact, Texas Gulf had made the copper-zinc discovery the previous November, but had kept the find secret in order to deter a land grab while carefully securing prospective ground in the immediate vicinity.

In mid-April, Texas Gulf attempted to squash the rumours by announcing that "the work done to date has not been sufficient to reach definite conclusions and any statement as to the size and grade of the ore would be premature and possibly misleading." But just four days later, under pressure to come clean, Texas Gulf issued the following release:

> Texas Sulpher Company has made a major discovery of zinc, copper, and silver in the Timmins area of Ontario Canada. This is a major discovery. Preliminary data indicate a reserve of more than 25 million tons of ore.

The news was distributed by telegram to newspapers and brokerage offices across the country. *The Northern Miner*, in exchange for secrecy, had been given an advance scoop so that a full story and accompanying editorial could be written in time for

the April 16th edition of the weekly paper. Shares of Texas Gulf —
which were trading at $17 when the hole was drilled — closed at
$37 dollars that day and eventually climbed to more than $170 as
confidence in the economics of the find grew.

Texas Gulf's first announcement, eerily similar to the release
issued a few months later by Windfall Oil and Mines, would
spawn a U.S. Securities & Exchange Commission investigation and
charges against Texas Gulf and 13 of its employees for issuing a
false and misleading press release and using information unavail-
able to the public to make personal profits. But, in the meantime,
the penny stock market was euphoric. The race to find the next
Kidd Creek was on.

Trading on the TSE the day after the release was described as
"hysterical" as volumes hit a new record. "The 30-million-share
activity caused the exchange's high-speed quotation ticker to be an
hour late in reporting floor transactions," reported *The Wall Street
Journal* on April 20. The story went on to say that "hotels, motels,
and any other rooming accommodations (in Timmins) are filled
(and) hardware stores are sold out of prospecting equipment. . . .
The only two brokerage houses in Timmins were so swamped on
Friday that potential customers were lined up in the streets."

One of the oldest clichés in the business is that "the best place to
find a mine is next to a mine." The saying refers to the tendency for
ore bodies, particularly the type represented by Kidd Creek, to occur
in clusters. For this reason, a major discovery invariably sparks a
staking rush by prospectors and companies eager to capitalize on the
potential for more deposits in the area. Companies with ground near
the discovery usually enjoy a bounce in their share price, regardless
of whether or not they conduct any exploration. It's an irresistible
way to make a quick buck for most promoters.

The Kidd Creek rush differed from conventional rushes
because of the lag time between the discovery (November 8, 1963)
and the public announcement of the discovery (April 16, 1964).
During this period, Texas Gulf staked an estimated 60,000 acres
under the supervision of geologist Kenneth Darke. But a handful of savvy prospectors, acting on rumours, also managed to

grab a considerable amount of land before Texas Gulf issued its announcement.

What was unknown at the time was that Darke was working both sides of the bush. In early 1964, while employed by Texas Gulf, he formed a partnership with two Timmins residents, Nedo Bragagnolo and John Angus, to stake mining claims as close as possible to the Texas Gulf discovery. Darke, either alone or with other Texas Gulf officials, had already dismissed these claims as unworthy of further examination. The partnership spent $7,000 staking the claims, then sold them for a total of $900,000 plus shares to unsuspecting purchasers and their investors. The Royal Commission investigation later exposed these property transactions as an example of how some prospectors and promoters used the speculative frenzy sparked by the Texas Gulf discovery for personal gain.

But Texas Gulf did leave behind some desirable claims in an otherwise thorough land acquisition program. Claim stakers often use aerial photographs to help them find their way around the bush and place claim posts accurately. In this case, the staker employed by Texas Gulf assumed, incorrectly, that a road on the photograph covering Prosser Township marked the southern boundary of the claims he intended to stake. As a result, four prospective claims were inadvertently left open, a fact that did not go unnoticed by an observant prospector named Don McKinnon, who promptly staked the claims for himself and his partners, John Larche and Fred Rousseau.

By the middle of April, 1964, the Larche-McKinnon-Rousseau partnership held 40 claims around Kidd Creek, including the four claims in Prosser Township that Texas Gulf had mistakenly left open. The fact that the Prosser claims contained an electromagnetic anomaly made them even more enticing. Although they often prove disappointing as harbingers of mineral wealth, electromagnetic anomalies indicate the presence of conductive or magnetic material under the surface. The Kidd Creek discovery hole had been spotted on just such an anomaly.

This combination of positive attributes piqued the interest of several potential buyers for the Prosser claims, including a scout from Noranda Explorations Limited, the exploration arm of the giant base metal producer Noranda Inc. The partnership gave Noranda right of first refusal on the land package, but the major rejected the option deal when another buyer expressed an interest in the claims. Waiting in the wings with an armload of cash was none other than Viola MacMillan.

QUEEN BEE STAKES HER CLAIM

On April 18th, MacMillan travelled to Timmins to meet Larche, who had worked on a number of her exploration jobs. After hours of negotiations in Larche's suite at the Empire Hotel that were interrupted briefly so that MacMillan could attend a dinner in nearby Schumacher, the two struck a deal at 1:30 the next morning. In exchange for three separate groups of four claims each, including the Prosser claim package, Larche and his partners would receive $100,000 cash on the spot plus 250,000 shares of Windfall Oils and Mines Limited owned by MacMillan. At the time, Windfall was trading at less than 40 cents per share. MacMillan agreed that the claims would be optioned to the junior company within 30 days. It was a remarkably sweet deal for the prospecting partnership.

As MacMillan states in her memoirs, she was especially interested in the four Prosser claims. Every promoter knows that in order to sell a property to investors, you have to spin a good story. What better story could there be than your company not only holds claims with a known electromagnetic anomaly near a major discovery, but that Texas Gulf would have had those claims for themselves if not for a staking error? In fact, a Texas Gulf representative later stated during the Royal Commission investigation that the company was not terribly concerned about the omission and wouldn't have paid more than $5,000 to get the claims back. If MacMillan knew this, she wasn't about to shout it from the treetops. The stage was set for some serious speculative activity in shares of Windfall Oil and Mines.

Although Windfall moved quickly to get the project underway, initial results proved disappointing. The anomaly MacMillan described as "one of the strongest known in the area" was estimated by the consulting geophysicist as being fourth order: in other words, not very strong at all. Nevertheless, he spotted the first hole on a 45-degree angle to intersect the anomaly at about 400 feet down the hole. Drilling began on July 1st and ended on Saturday morning, July 4th, at 570 ft. The sludge from the drill had turned black at the expected depth of the anomaly the night before, indicating that the drill had indeed entered conductive material. But was the black sludge potentially economic sulphide minerals or mere graphite?

Everyone was betting on the former. The Kidd Creek discovery had whetted the public's appetite for more strikes in the Timmins area and the chance to participate in the next "big one." Two of Canada's best-known and best-respected prospectors, George and Viola MacMillan, were drilling a property near the huge discovery and had paid a huge premium for the privilege. The Windfall claims contained an electromagnetic anomaly that could represent an extension of the Texas Gulf ore body, and the drill had apparently intersected that anomaly successfully. The drillers were already telling their friends in Timmins that Windfall had struck mineralization. Furthermore, George had removed several boxes of the core from the site to deter snoopers, a sure sign that the core contained valuable minerals. The rumour mill had the whole weekend to gather steam and by Monday it was ready to explode.

THE FRENZY BEGINS

"Some of the drillers started buying stock through their brokers, who would have told their other clients that if the drillers were buying, there must be something in the core. The market activity just blossomed from there, almost regardless of what the Mac-Millans did," says Ford. Blossomed is an understatement. On Monday morning, Windfall shares opened at $1.10. Before the market closed at 3:30 p.m., 1.57 million shares had changed hands and the price had reached $2. When rumours that the core contained 2.4% copper and 8% zinc surfaced later in the week, the trading accelerated and by the closing bell on July 10th, the price had doubled again to $4. "Such trading removed from the market any semblance of order and reduced it to a scene of uncontrollable speculative frenzy," observed Justice Arthur Kelly, the judge who presided over the Royal Commission.

In the absence of any concrete information, the press and brokerage houses latched onto rumour. They became enthusiastic boosters of the Windfall play, fuelling even more optimism in the market. *The Northern Miner* congratulated the "Mining MacMillans" for taking an intelligent gamble on the Prosser claims and *The New York Herald Tribune* reported a "major base metal drill core." Brokers added credence to the rumours by reporting them to investors as fact. "Frustrated by their efforts to get accurate information and feeling under compulsion to provide whatever information was available, (the brokers) gave out such reports as they were able to gather," concluded Justice Kelly. Just like during the Bre-X mining scandal that was to hit three decades later, the information mongers whose impartiality is so vital to the investing public were either unable or unwilling to see that the emperor was wearing no clothes.

Throughout this frenzy, the MacMillans kept their lips sealed save for two statements issued to the press on July 7th and again, under orders from the TSE, on July 15th. Both releases were equivocal, saying little more than that the first hole had been stopped at 530 feet, the core had not yet been sent for assay, and drilling would continue. The July 15th release read as follows:

> In view of the activity in the shares of Windfall Oil and Mines Limited over the past weeks, a meeting was held yesterday afternoon at the offices of the Ontario Securities Commission with the officials of the Company and of the Toronto Stock Exchange to review the situation.

At this discussion it was established, to the satisfaction of those present, that no assays of drill cores
taken from the property have been made to date.
No such assays have been made, since the first drill
hole of the Company had not yet been completed.
Any stories of assay results are unfounded and do
not come from the Company.

The Company advised that it will be recom-
mencing drilling shortly to complete the first hole.
When this drilling has been completed, the cores
will be assayed and the results announced forthwith. This work will take some time. To lessen the
possibility of rumours during the period of this
work all cores will be under guard. No information
will be released by the Company in regard to the
cores until the assays are completed.

There is little question that the MacMillans knew the core that had
intersected the target anomaly was worthless from the moment the
drillers pulled the core barrel out of the ground. George
MacMillan was an experienced prospector who would have been
able to determine from visual examination that the core was nearly
barren and the conductive material graphite, not sulfides. This
inescapable conclusion was reinforced several times throughout
the 23 days of market activity. On July 6th the MacMillans submitted two small pieces to Technical Service Laboratory in Toronto
and were told that the results showed nothing of value. Windfall's
consulting geologist, Dr. J.W. Ambrose, also had a chance to
examine the core on July 6th. A week later, he confirmed that his
tests revealed nothing of significance. Still, drilling resumed on July
18th even though the target zone had already been intersected.

George did not submit any samples for assay until July 24th,
more than two weeks after stopping the hole for the first time and
a day after completing the hole to 863 feet. According to witnesses
for the Royal Commission, he told Swastika Laboratories Ltd. to
take its time and report the assays by letter rather than phone.

Consequently, the public did not find out the core was worthless until the last day of July. "George knew what he was doing," says Brown. "He was quite capable of realizing there was nothing in the core. There was some fault or guilt in that."

Meanwhile, mainly during the first week of the market activity, Viola MacMillan was buying and selling shares of Windfall through her stable of junior companies, which collectively had the option to purchase 100,000 shares of Windfall at 40 cents and another 900,000 shares at 40–70 cents. Under a clause in the option agreement, the sudden rise in Windfall's share price compelled MacMillan to take up the shares or else forfeit the options. That day, her companies sold almost half a million shares at prices ranging from $1.01 to $2. Limited selling the next day was followed by modest purchases on July 8th. On July 9th, as rumours giving assay results of 2.4% copper and 8% zinc surfaced, MacMillan's companies sold another 333,200 shares as the price broke through the former high of $2.10. The same day, Ambrose tried to reach the MacMillans by telephone to convey the results of his testing. He left a message with the answering service, but never received a return phone call. On July 10th the companies sold an additional 73,400 shares at $3–4. By the time the market closed that day, the options had been exercised and the bulk of MacMillan's trading activity was complete.

The Royal Commission investigation, which — for the first time in Canadian history — had used a computer to analyze the Windfall trading activity, estimated MacMillan made a profit of $1.46 million on Windfall by trading though her controlled companies during July 1964. Losses by other investors totaled $2.7 million.

The TSE was partially to blame for this inequity. Throughout the heavy trading, the Exchange did virtually nothing to calm the frenzy or insist on disclosure that would confirm or deny the rumours swirling around Windfall. The only action the TSE took was to demand that Windfall disclose more accurate information about the mineral content of the drill core with the threat that if a satisfactory press release was not issued by July 13th, trading in Windfall would be suspended.

The TSE's attempt at enforcement was about as effective as the threats of an impotent schoolteacher wagging a finger at unruly students. Windfall's forced disclosure (see p. 193) was belated and vague, only serving to convince speculators that the company must have something big, since there was nothing in the release to suggest otherwise. The TSE did not suspend trading.

"The apparent acceptance of the uninformative statements, coupled with the fact that trading was permitted to continue, had the effect of confirming, in the public mind, confidence in the truthfulness of the rumours and creating the impression that something beyond the bare words of the statement had been made known to the Exchange officials, and that what the rumours alleged concerning the mineral worth of the core had been substantiated by the facts," concluded Justice Kelly. "The failure of the Exchange to take action earlier, and its failure to press to a conclusion of the action it threatened to take, can be explained only by . . . a reluctance to interfere with the continuance of trading."

CRACKDOWN

But how did a penny stock scandal — as common as a beehive hairdo in those days — lead to a royal commission, an investigation normally reserved for issues of major national or provincial importance?

First, there was the character at the centre of the investigation. MacMillan had a high profile not only among the general public, many of whom would remember her recent appearance on *To Tell the Truth*, but among the financial and political community. Although she was generally admired by her peers for her dedication to the mining industry and her work for the P.D.A., she had her detractors. "She had put a few people on the spot previously while trying to improve matters for the mining industry," says Tom Cole, a lawyer and former director of Windfall who handled most of MacMillan's business transactions. "She trod on quite a few toes."

Second, there were implications that several political figures, including Minister of Mines George Wardrope, were directly involved in the Windfall Affair. "One of the reasons Windfall was picked on was because there were a couple of newspaper stories about cabinet ministers being involved in the trading," says Justice Hartt. "The stories fueled the investigation, but we couldn't find any connection with the cabinet ministers at all." (OSC director John Campbell, however, was charged with breach of trust.)

Third, the trading volume was enormous by 1960s' standards — 13.3 million shares worth $36.7 million traded in 26,418 separate transactions — and the losses by the public substantial. "The rise in the market price of (Windfall's) shares during the month of July was almost unparalleled both in height and duration. The sudden drop in the price of its shares, when the long-delayed assays indicated the absence of any mineral of commercial value, left many investors poorer for the experience," wrote Justice Kelly in his final report. "There was inevitably much questioning as to how the loss occurred."

The commission involved 144 witnesses and 416 exhibits. About 80% of the 800 investors asked to give their opinion on speculative mining stocks in light of the Windfall Affair responded. After 44 days of hearings, Justice Kelly concluded that the TSE's efforts at self-regulation were woefully inadequate, that OSC director John Campbell's involvement in the trading was "shocking," and that the MacMillans were largely to blame for the run-up and subsequent crash in Windfall stock.

But the MacMillans defended the allegations against them using technically sound if not wholly believable arguments. They said they were merely following standard industry practice when they failed to disclose the results of their drilling program immediately. Well, yes and no.

George said he removed the core from the site not to feed the rumour mill, but to deter snoopers because there was no core shack on-site. This was a reasonable explanation. Members of the P.D.A. had recently been warned to lock up their core to ward off organized spies — including brokerage representatives and mining company personnel — seeking confidential information for stock market speculation. The OSC itself ordered Windfall to lock up the core on July 13, which only served to fuel expectations of a bonanza. "Nothing can create a market for you more than to have an official body put your core under lock and key," observes Ford.

The MacMillans also said it was standard practice to wait until a hole is finished to assay the core and release results to the public. True. Although it *is* unusual for a 900-foot hole to take a whole month to complete, companies usually finish at least one hole before sampling core and sending representative samples for assay.

Furthermore, although George was reprimanded for failing to disclose what he saw in the core, this type of visual examination without the support of assays is no longer considered acceptable for disclosure purposes. The current regulation was designed in the spirit of protecting investors from inflated estimates of value, not judgements of worthlessness, but is strictly enforced nonetheless. The conclusion reached by geological experts called by the Royal Commission was that there could be no question about the value of the Windfall core based on visual examination. But Ambrose — the Windfall consultant who himself had deemed the core worthless — defended the MacMillan's silence over the matter. "I have no intention of quibbling with my professional colleagues," he told the commission. "But to announce from a visual examination that a core contains no mineral value is merely an unsupported opinion until an assay is done."

As for her trading activity during the market run-up, MacMillan argued that as underwriter of the stock, she had a responsibility to maintain a stable market. The underwriting agreement gave her companies options on 100,000 Windfall shares at 40 cents and an additional 900,000 shares at prices of 40–70 cents. Under a clause in the agreement, she was forced to exercise these options by the rise in Windfall's stock price. The only way she could achieve the dual feat of maintaining a stable market and raising cash to cover the options, she argued, was to sell into the market. The average price at which she sold shares, either through her own account or through her controlled companies, was $2.06, although the stock frequently spiked above $4 and peaked at $5.65.

"The only way the MacMillans could control the market was

to sell into it to keep the market from becoming any more volatile than it already was," says Ford. "My overwhelming feeling on this, having known the MacMillans for so long, is that they weren't out to make money as a result of speculation. They wanted to find mines and they were successful to a large degree, and this was another one they hoped would turn out the same. I just can't accept, knowing them, that they tried to make something out of nothing. It just wasn't in their nature."

Justice Kelly took quite a different view. "The urge to distribute the underwritten and optioned stock made it undesirable that any positive statement as to the actual value be made while the distribution was going on. To complete the sale of the Windfall Company shares under option . . . it was necessary that the public be kept unaware of the negative results of the drilling," he wrote in his final report. "Without going into the fallacious reasoning upon which they justified their silence, the conclusion cannot be avoided that the uncertainty as to the truth or falsity of the rumours was deliberately allowed to continue, and that the elaborate security measures and the emphasis on the absence of assays were employed to perpetuate the belief that there was some factual basis for these rumours."

In 1965 George and Viola MacMillan were charged with defrauding the public by manipulating the shares of Windfall Oils and Mines. They would not be tried and acquitted for another four years.

In the meantime, more trouble lay ahead for Viola MacMillan, who by then had resigned as president of the P.D.A. to avoid smearing the organization. The unprecedented use of computers to analyze some 26,000 stock transactions during the Commission investigation had inadvertently revealed that one day in July, MacMillan bought and sold several thousand shares of Consolidated Golden Arrow Mines Ltd., one of her junior companies that held a stake in Windfall.

Just before the market opened on July 10th, MacMillan told her broker to sell 244,000 shares of Golden Arrow on behalf of two of her companies and buy the same number of shares for friends and neighbours. Specifically, she asked the broker to sell 44,000 shares for Airquests Ltd. at 25 cents per share and buy 44,000 shares for nine individuals at 25 cents per share. She also instructed him to sell 200,000 shares held by MacMillan Prospecting & Development Co. Ltd. for 25 cents per share and buy the same amount at the same price for George.

About an hour after the market opened, Viola called the broker again, asked him what Golden Arrow was trading at and, after hearing the stock price had jumped to 58–65 cents, told him to sell a total of 6,000 shares for the nine individuals. Later in the day, she instructed him to sell 10,000 shares for George at 64–65 cents per share for a profit of about $4,000. The total trades in Golden Arrow on July 10th amounted to 393,000 shares, compared with just 850 shares the previous day.

The huge volume of single day trading leapt off the computer screen and raised a red flag for commission investigators. Even though she did not benefit personally from the trades, MacMillan was charged and convicted of wash trading — the act of buying and selling large blocks of a stock in order to create a false or misleading appearance of market activity. Neither she nor George testified at her subsequent trial. She was sentenced to a nine-month jail term, fined $10,000, and — at the age of 64 — escorted to Toronto's Don Jail. Her appeal was unsuccessful, but for once MacMillan's gender worked in her favour. The appeal judge changed the sentence to an "indefinite period not exceeding nine months" because "the appellant is female." This slight change in wording opened the doors for MacMillan's early release.

MacMillan's wash trading conviction was the first in Canadian history. The OSC had tried to convict the promoters of Avonic Mining twice in 1957 but both trials resulted in a hung jury based on the argument that the public didn't get hurt. "Viola had just been convicted of a practice that is almost as common, but just as illegal in Canada, as contraception," wrote Cameron Darby in *Saturday Night*. "She was simply behaving like your average billionaire promoter, operating a business, which, with government acquiescence, has always been 10% production and 90% piracy." The judge, also calling the trading an "act of piracy," ruled that a jail term was necessary because a fine alone would be regarded as a licence to continue such trades.

There are many theories about why MacMillan was convicted of a crime otherwise overlooked. Some say there was lingering resentment towards MacMillan, as a woman, for assuming she could take such an esteemed position in a man's world. Others argue that MacMillan sealed her own fate by making enemies on Bay Street and in government circles as an outspoken advocate for her own interests and for those of the industry. Some question the strength of her legal defence. Observers also point to a strong feeling among the public that someone had to take the blame for the money lost on Windfall and other properties surrounding the Texas Gulf discovery. With all these cards stacked against her, MacMillan was a sitting duck when the computer analysis highlighted her unusual trading activity of July 10, 1964.

Stock price manipulation remains a murky area for market regulators. In 2000, portfolio managers and traders at RT Capital Management, the Royal Bank of Canada's pension management arm, allegedly conspired to enhance their performance numbers by manipulating stock values at the end of the day using a practice called "high closing." The OSC fined the Royal Bank $3 million and the TSE suspended 12 traders and fined them a total of $360,000. The charges stunned the financial industry because high closing, like wash trading in the 1960s, was accepted as common practice. In both cases, a shift in regulatory attitude prompted the authorities to take action against individuals in order to send a message to the whole industry about tolerance for unethical practices.

BEHIND BARS

During her incarceration at the Women's Guidance Centre in Ingleside, Ontario, Viola and George exchanged letters almost daily. Viola's letters are, unsurprisingly, laden with instructions regarding the couple's various accounts, companies, and residences. It was perhaps the first time in her life that MacMillan felt truly impotent, and she had difficulty ceding control over her business matters to George. She had flashes of anguish and indignation over her fate. "It will be hard for me to catch up and orient myself back to that wonderful record I had before this dreadful mess," she writes shortly after her incarceration. And later: "I have moments when all my hard work and achievements come tumbling down and I think of all the rascals getting away with so much. . . . I am praying that I will be released soon. . . . Surely they have had their pound of flesh." She often cried herself to sleep.

But the "Old Vi," that optimistic dynamo that thrived on adversity, penetrated the gloom whenever MacMillan contemplated her release. "After this very unpleasant experience, I'm sure our lives will be richer and fuller," she reassures George. "I'm sure there will be still time left in our lives for us to do some good and be a friend to man." She even instructed George to keep his ear to the ground for exploration opportunities because she was anxious to find another mine. Ever conscious of her public appearance, she gave George a specific list of clothes and accessories she would need for her release. She may have been the first and last prisoner at the Women's Guidance Centre to request that a fur coat be brought to her jail cell.

MacMillan also comes across as religious and empathetic in her letters. She took visits from various clergy and prayed often, actions which may have helped her secure an early release, since three of the questions on the parole application inquired about religious affiliation and church-going habits. Despite her own worries, her letters were sprinkled with references and messages of goodwill to others who were suffering from illness or anxiety. She clearly missed George and frequently referred to the good times they had and would have together. "Did I tell you that I'm still in love with you?" she asked at the opening on one dispatch. But she rarely referred to her conviction or expressed any kind of remorse for her actions other than to ask George "where did we fail?"

During her incarceration, a cast of characters was working feverishly behind the scenes to secure her early release. Most of the arguments for her parole revolved around her age (64), her frail health (she had a heart condition), and her reputation preceding the conviction. MacMillan had befriended some powerful people in business and politics, including Kelso Roberts, former attorney general of Ontario and Vera Conant, the widow of former Ontario Premier Gordon Conant. Her trial lawyer, Joseph Sedgwick, was quick to offer these alliances with "highly reputable citizens" as proof of her good character.

Tom Cole, MacMillan's long-time solicitor, wrote a personal appeal saying he believed MacMillan had "no idea that she was breaking the law" when she traded the Golden Arrow shares. "It follows, naturally, that I do not believe detention is going to affect a non-existing propensity to crime," he wrote to Frank Potts, chairman of the Ontario Parole Board. The campaign worked and MacMillan was released on parole after serving only seven weeks of her nine-month sentence.

The early release angered many who felt that MacMillan was given special treatment because she was wealthy. At the time, there was a loose policy that inmates with an outstanding charge, such as MacMillan's fraud allegation, should be denied parole until the other charge was heard. "It is intolerable that there should be different rules for the rich and the poor in this province," said Morton Shulman, then an NDP member of the provincial legislature. But Shulman's protest fell on mostly deaf ears as MacMillan amassed an expert legal team, including Kelso Roberts, to defend her against the fraud charges.

On February 10, 1969, almost a year after Viola's release from jail on the wash trading conviction, George and Viola MacMillan were acquitted on both counts of fraud. Judge Harry Deyman said he could find no evidence that they had influenced the price of or falsely promoted Windfall stock. He said that the Texas Gulf discovery combined with a large volume of buy orders from the Timmins area on the weekend of July 4–5th, 1964, were to blame for the rapid acceleration in Windfall's share price. Furthermore, the judge said he could find nothing fraudulent in the MacMillans' statements to the press on July 6th and July 15th, even though the Crown alleged that the couple could have done more to quell rumours about the value of the core. "The MacMillans didn't deceive anyone. I can't find their action in waiting for a core assay wrong," Deyman told the courtroom.

THE DOMINO EFFECT

The Windfall Affair was to have repercussions far beyond destroying the MacMillans' reputation. The Royal Commission investigation uncovered serious weaknesses in the regulatory practices of the TSE, which had approved Windfall's ambiguous release of July 15th and failed to suspend trading in shares of the company during the speculative frenzy. Justice Kelly questioned whether the exchange functioned as a watchdog or as a "private gaming club" designed to line the pockets of some of its associates.

The OSC also came under attack. "What was the Securities Commission doing, if anything, during this episode?" asked Joubin, the famous geologist cum prospector, in a memo to Justice Kelly regarding the Windfall Affair. "If they were active, results certainly indicate that they were not effective! Why not? Who should be effective in such cases? Does anyone know?" OSC director John Campbell's simple explanation was: "You just don't go to Viola and say 'I want this' or 'we are going to do this.' I mean, you just don't do that to Viola MacMillan." Campbell was suspended for his involvement in Windfall trading and later resigned from the civil service altogether.

So, in a perverse sense, the MacMillans did the investing public a favour. A new and improved Securities Act came into force with the relationship between the OSC and TSE more clearly defined. The TSE cleaned house and discouraged new speculative stock listings by introducing tougher rules for junior oil and mining companies. "Toronto was planning to clean up its act," recalls Brown. "They wanted the blue chip stocks in and the scoundrels out." There was a "sea change" in the stock market, agrees Frank Kaplan, reporter for *The Financial Post* during the Windfall Affair. "The securities commission and the stock exchange felt that they had been very badly misled by Bay Street," he says. "They started to use the regulations to prosecute aggressively."

As a result, many of the penny stocks and their promoters moved to the Vancouver Stock Exchange (VSE), which welcomed the new business. "Between 1964 and 1967 the backbone of the Toronto penny stock market, the sharp-eyed, quick-tongued promoters, masters of hyperbole, slid into Vancouver en masse," wrote authors David Cruise and Alison Griffiths in *Fleecing the Lamb*. Toronto became staid, conservative, and blue chip. Vancouver became the new Wild West.

The P.D.A. also went down with MacMillan. The organization that she had toiled so long and so hard to build crumbled under the weight of the Windfall allegations. All prospectors and promoters were painted with the same brush. "The P.D.A. association virtually fell apart," says Kaplan. "No one wanted to have anything to do with it, and the big companies wouldn't let their people go to the annual convention. A few guys kept it going with great difficulty." The P.D.A. would eventually recover its strength and respectability, but it would take several years of mostly volunteer work to repair the damage done by Windfall.

The Windfall court appearance was to be Viola MacMillan's last public outing for some time. "She went totally underground," says Kaplan. The dreams of finding another mine that sustained her through her darkest days in jail never came true. She and George tried to get some new ventures going after her release from jail, but none of them panned out. She was forgotten by the press and felt shunned by many of her former colleagues. She lost George in 1978. Her other love, the mining industry, mirrored her demise. Penny stocks fell out of favour with investors, at least temporarily, and bigger companies — with the exception of gold producers — were battered by low metal prices throughout much of the '70s and '80s.

PARDON CLEANS THE SLATE

But supporters continued to work behind the scenes to restore MacMillan's reputation. In 1978, about two weeks after George's death, MacMillan received a pardon for her wash trading conviction from the federal government. "This pardon is evidence of the fact that the National Parole Board, after making proper inquiries, was satisfied that the said Viola Rita MacMillan, nee Viola Rita Huggard, was of good behaviour and that the conviction should no longer reflect adversely on her character," the document reads.

A pardon in Canada does not imply that the conviction was misguided, but rather that the convicted deserves to carry on without the shadow of past offences blocking the way to employment and other benefits. "It has everything to do with the nature of the person," says Tom Cole, who was instrumental in securing the pardon. "A lot of people felt a little later like she'd had a pretty raw deal, and I think that was also relevant." MacMillan kept the pardon a secret, sealing the actual statement in an envelope marked "not to be opened until my death." Although the news did leak out before she died, she considered the conviction and subsequent pardon "one of those closed subjects that she didn't want to talk about," says close friend Thelma Brown.

Perhaps emboldened by her pardon, MacMillan began to step out gingerly for the first time in years. Kaplan remembers giving a speech at a P.D.A. convention luncheon in March, 1980, and spotting MacMillan in the crowd. He believes this was the first time she had appeared at a mining function since being released from jail in 1968.

If the pardon helped MacMillan recover her private dignity, her donation to the Museum of Nature in Ottawa did wonders for her public reputation. In 1989 she pledged $1.25 million — almost as much as her profit on Windfall — to help the museum purchase the William Pinch mineral collection, a spectacular assembly of 16,000 mineral specimens considered among the top five of its kind in the world. In recognition of her generous donation, the museum named the collection the Viola MacMillan Mineral Gallery. "With her donation, (MacMillan) has helped ensure that all Canadians will have the opportunity to share in her passion," said the Pinch campaign newsletter.

Following the purchase of the Pinch collection, MacMillan was inducted into the Canadian Mining Hall of Fame and became a member of the Order of Canada on her 90th birthday. "Viola

MacMillan had two careers in the mining industry. First, over a period that spanned four decades, she and her husband teamed up as prospectors and developers of several substantial mineral deposits across the country. Her success as a mine finder and financier was substantial, but she was also the driving force behind the transformation of a small, regional association of prospectors into an internationally recognized association of professionals involved in all aspects of mineral exploration in Canada," her Hall of Fame citation reads.

On August 26, 1993, just four months after her Order of Canada investiture, MacMillan collapsed on her way to the bank. She was rushed to the hospital but couldn't be revived. Joubin, who had become her closest companion in her final years but could not claim to be a relative, was barred from her hospital room. She died of a heart attack at the age of 90, alone but not forgotten.

Only MacMillan knew for certain if she acted out of self-interest during that fateful summer in 1964. But regardless of her motivation, there is general agreement that her actions are less damning when viewed in the context of the stock market culture at the time. The whole market was badly regulated and prone to manipulation, particularly around the time of the Kidd Creek find, but Windfall was picked on because MacMillan's high profile and the possible involvement of powerful politicians made for an especially compelling case. "All the penny stocks were going wild and there were bucket shops up and down Bay Street. It was within that atmosphere that Windfall took place," says Justice Hartt. "I think the Royal Commission operated strictly in isolation, out of context of what was happening on Bay Street."

REFERENCES

Joubin, Franc R. and D. McCormack Smyth. *Not for Gold Alone: The Memoirs of a Prospector*. Toronto: Deljay Publications, 1986.

Cruise, David and Alison Griffiths. *Fleecing the Lamb: The Inside Story of the Vancouver Stock Exchange*. Vancouver: Douglas & McIntyre, 1987.

Shulman, Morton. *The Billion Dollar Windfall*. Toronto: McGraw Hill, 1969.

Canadian Museum of Nature. Viola MacMillan Papers. Ottawa, 1995. [Viola's letters to George.]

Croft, Roger. *Swindle! A Decade of Canadian Stock Frauds*. Toronto: Gage Publishing, 1975.

Darby, Cameron. "Viola and the Toronto Stock Exchange," *Saturday Night*, May 1967.

Lonn, George. *Men and Mines: Short Biographies of Some Colorful Contemporary Figures behind Canada's Mighty Mining Industry*. Toronto: Pitt Publishing, 1962.

McCall, Christina. "The Prospector in the Pink Penthouse," *Maclean's*, July 20, 1957.

PHOTO CREDITS